CALLED TO SERVE

A BIBLICAL INVITATION TO
SACRIFICIAL SERVANTHOOD

ENDORSEMENTS

Called to Serve addresses a most urgent and pressing need throughout the Christian world for more leaders who are committed to following the example of Christ, who came not to be ministered to, but to minister and to give His life as a ransom for many. Patrick Muriithi's reflections, enhanced by his sharing of his own struggles, victories, and relevant anecdotal illustrations, shows the reader what it really means to follow Christ and to lead others to do the same.

Dr John Anonby
Author, *The Kenyan Epic Novelist Ngugi*
Canada

Once I started reading this book, I couldn't put it down. Powered by an impassioned commitment to servanthood, Patrick writes with insight and a refreshing ability to tell stories. And best of all, I finished the book, not just knowing what it means to serve but believing that God can make even a self-serving man like me a servant.

Bill Perkins
Author of *Six Battles Every Man Must Win* and
When Good Men Get Angry
USA

Patrick has taken on the important, yet much ignored, subject of servanthood and has done it in a way that will both challenge and train your heart for service. You cannot read through these pages and remain 'lukewarm'. If you are after some real change, and not just some temporary relief, this is the book for you.

Pastor Bill McKisic
Church on the Summit
Cleveland, Ohio, USA

The principles shared in this book describe who Patrick is: a genuine servant. From my interaction with him in ministry, I can testify he has lived, practiced, demonstrated, and taught these principles, and now has written them down. I have seen the spirit of servanthood raise Patrick from the village to an international minister of the gospel.

Prophet Paul Mwaniki
GCC Church
Nanyuki, Kenya

In *Called to Serve*, Patrick has shared with us his heartbeat and practice of ministry. I recommend this book to anyone who wants to follow what Christ teaches— servanthood—the only tested and proven principle for successful leadership.

Dr Kirimi Barine
Author & Publisher
Nairobi, Kenya

I have known Patrick as a man of integrity, humility, And a passionate servant leader. He is not an armchair-general; he truly has practiced and lives out the principles laid out in *Called to Serve*. Read this book to know the great wealth of wisdom that leads to servanthood.

Dr Collins Chipaya
Founder and Presiding Apostle, Revival Fire Missions
International
Zambia

The greatest form of worship is service to God. Not only is this book a great inspiration, but an insightful wealth of knowledge into what is every human being's divine purpose as taught by the greatest Bible teacher I have ever come across.

Hon Karimi Njeru
Magistrate

Since the kingdom of God requires great servant leaders, Called to Serve presents to the reader a truth that when practiced, will produce a kingdom labour-force that will impact the body of Christ and society at large. Apostle Patrick Muriithi presents the subject of service with not only life-changing stories but also with his own exemplary life. I highly recommend this book for the training of workers in every church everywhere.

Dr David Juma
Founder and Apostle,
Life Church International

This book is a true depiction of Apostle Patrick's servant heart. It is written for other servants who are willing to live to the calling they have received through Christ Jesus. The realisation that we have been called to serve in power and integrity without compromising, is an unending echo that is left lingering in our hearts even after keeping the book down.

Evangelist Noel Ngure
Founder, Beyond Horizons International &
Daughters of Faith Ministries,
USA

This book is an authentic lifestyle of the writer Apostle Patrick Muriithi. He is a true servant who has gone through the various obstacles and tests of service to the zone of enjoying the rewards of his faithfulness in Service. The Book comes at a critical time when everyone wants to be served but Apostle Patrick is a servant leader who put other people's needs, aspiration and interest above his own. As a servant leader, Apostle Patrick does not force people to follow, but walks with them, and moves in a direction that unites all in a common vision. This is a must read for emerging leaders who aspire to be followed.

Bishop Jackson Kingori
Dallas, Texas, USA

I read my friends book, _Called to Serve,_ straight through without putting it down! It has reignited me and inspired me to serve in a sacrificial manner. Apostle Patrick is an anointed author and I recommend this book to everyone.

Jason Norton
Senior Pastor, Kings Trail Cowboy Church
Texas, USA

CALLED TO SERVE

A BIBLICAL INVITATION TO SACRIFICIAL SERVANTHOOD

PATRICK MURIITHI NYAGA

PUBLISHING
Institute of Africa

CALLED TO SERVE: A Biblical Invitation to Sacrificial Servanthood

Copyright © 2009 Patrick Muriithi Nyaga

Revised and updated © 2020

All rights reserved. No part of this book may be reproduced in any form, except for the inclusion of brief quotations in a review, without permission in writing from the publisher.

ISBN 13: 978-9966-69-046-3

This edition published by:

PUBLISHING
Institute of Africa

P.O. Box 16458 - 00100
NAIROBI. KENYA
info@publishing-institute.org
www.publishing-institute.org

Originally published by Integrity Publishers Inc., USA.

Unless otherwise indicated, Scripture quotations are taken from the New King James Version®. Copyright © 1982 by Thomas Nelson. Used by permission. All rights reserved.

CONTENTS

Dedication ix

Foreword xiii

Special Thanks xv

Introduction xvii

1   The Call to Serve 1

2   Qualities of a Servant 17

3   Servants' Attitude 29

4   Obstacles to Service 41

5   Servants' Tests 55

6   Servants' Rewards 61

Conclusion 73

Bibliography 77

I dedicate this book to my parents: my late dad, Nyaga, and Lucy, who raised me in the fear of the Lord and, by faith, prophesied over my life when they named me Muriithi (shepherd). The prophecy came true, for I am now a shepherd of the Lord's flock.

For even the Son of Man did not come to be served, but to serve, and to give His life a ransom for many.

Mark 10:45

FOREWORD

In the Old Testament, the elders understood that servanthood was the key to staying in leadership: '…If today you will be a servant to these people and serve them and give them a favourable answer, they will always be your servants' (1 Kings 12:7, NIV). In the New Testament, Jesus Christ is the best model of servanthood: '…the Son of Man did not come to be served, but to serve, and to give his life as a ransom for many'(Matthew 20:28, NIV). The way to greatness, therefore, is in serving others rather than expecting to be served (Matthew 20:26,27).

Called to Serve demonstrates the beauty and benefits of being a servant. We have come to view service as tiresome and an interruption. Service is the vehicle to self-sufficiency, health, promotion, and honour. Even though serving others is demanding, the blessings that come with service far outweigh the sacrifice and should motivate us to serve.

Patrick has taught the principles set forth in this book wherever we have started churches and the results have always been the same— vibrant people who work zealously for God. Service is the antidote for pride and the door to God's blessings.

I recommend this book for those seeking to understand how to please God. Service will not only bring positive change to your life and ministry but also joy and freedom.

God's Word expressly teaches about sacrificial service; it is the vehicle to your promotion and gateway to blessings. Try service as a way of life and you will never have to seek for blessings; they will follow you instead.

Dr Sammy Gitaari
Bishop, Gospel Celebration Church

SPECIAL THANKS

To my Lord Jesus Christ, the ultimate servant leader, for His strength, and the revelation He gives.

To my wife, Grace, whose support made sure this book was born. Thank you for being so understanding and not complaining as I worked on this book into the wee hours of the night.

To my daughter Jewel and my sons Moses and Collins, the all-time recipients of my servanthood. You encourage me daily through your smiles and love.

To the Gospel Celebration Church family, for accepting my ministry and giving me a platform to exercise servanthood.

INTRODUCTION

The cry of God for servants can still be heard. Like it was in the days of prophet Isaiah, God asks, '...Whom shall I send and who will go for us?' (Isaiah 6:8). Many rogue servants of God, have ruined lives, businesses, and families as they purport to serve God, yet do not. Often, these servants started well but veered off the way for various reasons (Galatians 3:3).

People have the notion that to be God's servant, you must be clergy or in the fivefold ministry. You can serve God whether you clean washrooms or head a corporate team. I have served God in different areas and have enjoyed great benefits that I share in this book.

But is there reward in service? There is nothing wrong in asking this question. Peter asked it to Jesus, '...We've given up everything to follow you. What will we get?' (Matthew 19:27, NLT). The devil also asked God a similar question concerning Job. Does Job fear [serve] you for nothing? (Job 1:9). What is the reward for service? This book will seek to answer this question. Over the years, God has shown me that servants for His kingdom are in short supply. Many are in ministry for different reasons, including building their CV's to prepare themselves for greener pastures elsewhere; few are servants.

One time, while attending a funeral service with a friend, a drunkard, looking beaten and emaciated sat opposite us. My friend whispered to me that he and that man were agemates. It was unbelievable for there was nothing similar between the two. So I asked him the secret of staying young and he told me, 'Serve God even in the most simple way and you will be preserved'. Jesus demonstrated clearly that He came to serve and not to be served. This book will help the servant know how to serve without giving up or looking for people's commendations or rewards.

Called to Serve is simple, practical, and relevant for anyone serving in any level of ministry. It is a tool that leaders can reference as they teach God's people the road to servanthood. I pray that as you read this book, your eyes of understanding will open, and you will respond to God's call to sacrificial servanthood.

CHAPTER ONE

THE CALL TO SERVE

And the LORD spoke to Moses, 'Go to Pharaoh and say to him, "Thus says the LORD: Let My people go, that they may serve Me."' (Exodus 8:1).

I once shared the gospel with an acquaintance who blatantly refused to surrender his life to Jesus as saviour. Some years later, I met him, and he shared the joy of salvation and his turnaround story. It was a blessing hearing his testimony and God's work of transformation. Then I asked him, 'Why did you decide to get saved when you did and not when I preached to you?' With a smile he replied, 'You never gave me an actual reason to be saved. I did not see the sense of salvation only to go to heaven. I could not imagine waiting for someone I could not see coming from a place I did not know. Life would be so boring. When I discovered that salvation is about service, it was an easy decision: for I got saved to serve.'

This man was right in saying I never gave him a good reason to be saved. I did not tell him that salvation is also an enrolment to the service of the King. Imagine how many people are not inclined towards salvation for the sole reason that it is 'boring'. Could you be among those propagating this kind of gospel, if not audibly, then through your lifestyle? We are called to serve.

God is on the lookout for people who will serve Him. The Scriptures show clearly that whenever God called anyone to 'work for Him', they were busy serving somewhere. God is not looking for idlers. Peter was fishing, Matthew was collecting taxes, Elisha was a committed farmer, and Gideon was winnowing his wheat. If God will use me, He should not find me sitting idle.

At the same time, service does not mean merely being busy. There are many busy people who can never account for their time or show the output of their efforts and energy. Worse still, many have no plans. They are like firefighters who can never plan their work. Their diaries are typically blank, just waiting for emergencies. Every Christian should know that God did not save them only to go to heaven but to serve Him on earth too.

Let my people go, that they may serve me (Exodus 8:1).

It is amazing to see the reason God wanted to free His people. God did not set the Israelites free because they were in captivity; the Bible tells us He set them free to serve Him. He did not expect His children to serve Him while in bondage; He had to first set them free. Apostle Paul talks to Timothy about being a soldier (2 Timothy 2:3-4). Apart from the uniform and discipline of a soldier, the next distinguishing aspect is service. Soldiers do not just lay back and wait for the month to end and then demand their pay. They are always in service. Though a salary may be the reward for their work, service is the language they understand. An individual would not last long in the military if the only reason for enlisting were a pay cheque.

I grew up with the dream that one day I would become a soldier. I often prayed that God would grant me this desire. Unfortunately, when I gave my life to Jesus, I received a discouraging message from a friend: he told me I could never realise my dream since one requirement in the forces was that one had to take drugs like bhang (cannabis) to work effectively. I did not want to compromise my faith, so I dropped that dream.

Many years later, a paramilitary police officer debunked this myth and provided the proper perspective about working in the military. 'Pastor, the fact is, we love our work and may not take any kind of intoxicating substance for any motivational reasons. Our training is to handle criminals and to keep law and order.' This tells us that service demands calling, training, and discipline.

Many people today are looking for people to serve them. God doesn't call us to be served but to serve. May the Lord help us change our attitude towards service! Jesus, being God, became a servant, humbled Himself even to the point of death. He washed His disciples' feet and offered Himself as a sacrifice for you and me. We cannot achieve much for God if we will not deny ourselves, take up our cross, and follow Him (Matthew 16:24).

Becoming a True Servant

Servanthood demands that we ought to go all the way in obedience to the Word of God. Servanthood can be compared to athletics. An athlete must work on their speed, fitness, and technique, among other requirements, to increase their chances of winning. An athlete who only works on one thing may not win in a highly competitive environment. They have to be involved in comprehensive training and are expected to train and practice daily. As servants, we must 'work out our salvation with fear and trembling' (Philippians 2:12).

Servanthood is about sacrifice. Just like the Bible says that many are called, but few are chosen (Matthew 22:14), I would say, many are serving, but few are serving sacrificially. Sacrificial servanthood is seen in the level of self-denial a person is willing to make for the sake of another. A servant leader must be willing to sacrifice something for the benefit of the people they lead. Paul wrote to the Romans making a plea for them to offer their bodies as living sacrifices. 'I beseech you therefore, brethren, by the mercies of God, that you present your bodies a living sacrifice, holy, acceptable to God, which is your reasonable service' (Romans 12:1).

Paul knew what the Law of Moses prescribed as an acceptable sacrifice and thus did not expect the believers to burn their bodies on an altar. I believe Paul desired for the Roman Church to see the call to servanthood through the eye of the Old Testament expectations of a sacrifice. Let us look at some of these requirements.

A SACRIFICE MUST BE CHOSEN

In the Old Testament, sacrifices were chosen as per God's specifications, the people did not dictate what they would sacrifice to God. When one senses the call to serve God, they must recognise that God has chosen them.

'But you, O Israel, my servant, Jacob, whom I have chosen, you descendants of Abraham my friend, I took you from the ends of the earth from its furthest corners I called you, I said you are my servant; I have chosen and have not rejected you' (Isaiah 41:8-9, NIV).

God is almighty and knows everything. He chooses us and we follow Him. Since we belong to Him, He reveals His special plan for us and defines our boundaries. This means that we might have to lose some friends or forfeit certain job opportunities, but this loss does not supersede the fact that when we are born again, we are chosen to join the royal priesthood of chosen people and to be a sacrifice, made holy by the blood of Jesus (1 Peter 2:9). I am so glad that the almighty God chose me and saved me through His Son, Jesus Christ.

'Then God said, "Take your son, your only son, whom you love—Isaac—and go to the region of Moriah. Sacrifice him there as a burnt offering on a mountain I will show you' (Genesis 22:2, NIV).

God was very specific and clear about the kind of sacrifice He required from Abraham. Given free will, like any reasonable human being, Abraham would not have voluntarily chosen to sacrifice Isaac. But in obedience to God's Word, he heeded the instruction. How often do we make sacrifices to God, without consulting on His particular choice?

Abraham had only one son, one he loved deeply, but he was willing to sacrifice him in obedience to God's Word. God sacrificed His only Son for us. When Elijah asked the widow of Zarephath to bring him water to drink, the request seemed manageable; but when he asked for bread, this request would come at a cost, yet the widow obeyed the prophet's word (1Kings 17:10-12). You do not sacrifice because you have much or out of abundance; you sacrifice because you acknowledge who God is and in obedience to His Word.

A story is told of a man who owned an ewe. He made God this promise, 'God, when this sheep gives birth, I promise to offer the lamb to my church as my sacrifice to you'. God heard his prayer and did more than the man asked. The ewe gave birth to twins. 'One of these lambs belongs to God' the man said but never specified which one. After a few months, one lamb died. The man prayed, 'Oh God, I am sorry your lamb died.' If God chose us and did not spare His only Son for our sake, then we ought to let our own sacrifice to Him cost us.

A SACRIFICE MUST BE SET APART

Many of us are ready to serve God and walk with Him, but we are not ready to be set apart. When God accepts you as a sacrifice, He sets you apart. In other words, He separates us for a noble cause.

'The Lord had said to Abram, leave your country, your people and your father's household and go to the land I will show you. I will make you into a great nation and I will bless you; I will make your name great, and you will be a blessing' (Genesis 12:1).

God demanded separation from Abram. As we desire servanthood, we must be willing to separate. Failure to separate will always put us in a place of compromise. There are many new things God wants to do in and with us if only we would say, 'Lord, I agree to separate'. We must be willing to set ourselves apart. God knew that it would be hard for Abram to obey Him while he remained with his own people and culture, that is why He told him to leave everything behind and follow His leading.

It is not easy to detach ourselves from people, places, and things, but God demands it from us. Abram opted to take his nephew Lot along with him. This was not God's instruction. No wonder Abram and Lot reached a point of disagreement that led to separation. Separation is a sacrificial step in servanthood. Leaving the people or things we love in obedience to the Word of God is not easy, but God demands it.

I will never forget the day I decided to give my life to Jesus. The Christian Union in high school usually organised sessions during the term of continuous worship and word, dubbed 'weekend challenge'. I came into the hall and sat at the back with some naughty friends as the preaching went on. We were making noise and mocking the preacher as he spoke. The preacher soon demanded silence from the audience as he asked those who desired to get saved to raise their hands. I immediately felt the Holy Spirit convict me of my sins and I decided to get saved. Surrounded by my friends, I lifted my hand to receive Jesus. At once, the friend next to me promptly pulled down my hand saying, 'Patrick, you can't get saved.' That night I never slept. The following day when I went for the meeting, I did not sit at the back with my friends, I went straight to the front row. I separated myself. When the preacher called for those who wanted to get saved, I never lifted my hand; I walked to the front and knelt. I had to separate myself from my friends; I had to sacrifice my relationships for the sake of Christ. God needs our maximum attention. There are many things that can hinder us from hearing His voice. Since God is interested in our fellowship, He makes sure we are strategically positioned to hear Him. It is right to say that great ministries blossom in the wilderness, a place for maximum attention. Jesus spent forty days and nights in the wilderness before starting His ministry. David stayed in the desert for years even though he was an anointed king. In the wilderness you will give to God your full attention.

> *By faith Moses, when he became of age, refused to be called the son of Pharaoh's daughter* (Hebrews 11:24).

Moses separated himself from the pleasures of the palace and instead went to suffer with his own people. If Moses were to come to you for advice, you might have advised him not to abandon the palace or perhaps ask if he would recommend you to pharaoh to take his place. Moses left a life of plenty and chose to work as a shepherd. One day the Lord appeared to him in a burning bush. It would have been difficult for Moses to hear and obey God in his comfort zone—the palace. When it is time to separate, God does not expect you to look for logic, He expects you to obey.

You might be going through your own wilderness as a result of separation. Do not give up; joy comes in the morning. A bush is about to burn and God will give you direction. Do not complain, God is in the process of equipping and perfecting you. If you want to know where God is taking you, look at what He is taking you through. Remember, the height of a building is determined by the depth of its foundation, the bigger the assignment, the harder the training.

A SACRIFICE MUST DIE

Before you sacrifice an animal, however small, you have to kill it first. In the same way, if we have to serve God sacrificially, we must be willing to die. When we were growing up, my mother once asked me to slaughter a chicken for supper. In my childish thoughts and wanting to be mischievous, I boiled the water and figured I would take a shortcut and put the live bird into the pot of boiling water meant for plucking the chicken's feathers. The idea seemed great to me and I proceeded to do exactly that. There are no words to explain what happened next. By the time I realised what was going on, the village boys had gathered around in response to my screams. The chicken was nowhere to be found, which by itself was a tragedy, and on top of that, I had severe burns from the boiling water. We can only imagine what the result would be of trying to get a larger animal such as a goat or sheep to cooperate with being sacrificed while still alive! From my experience, I learnt it is dangerous to sacrifice a living animal. To do so can only mean you will most likely keep rebuilding your altars because your sacrifices will always escape.

In the many years I have served in ministry, I have seen the frustrations and difficulties people experience when they want to be sacrifices to God, but at the same time do not want to die to some things. Unless the Lord builds the house, the builders labour in vain (Psalm 127:1). Becoming a sacrifice that is holy and acceptable to God will bring pain and hurt. There are many things to be sacrificed on the altar—anger, hatred, bitterness, insults, lust, unforgiveness, slander, and malice. If these things are alive in you, however much you want to be a sacrifice to God, you will end up jumping out of the altar.

Serving God is not a smooth ride. There are times things get difficult. Sometimes the people you serve can turn against you. They turned against Jesus and crucified Him after He healed their sick and fed them with bread. As a pastor, I know too well that one of the most unthankful institutions to serve in is the church. Once you fall out of favour with members, they will rarely remember your good days. I have seen pastors cry with bitterness remembering how they served a congregation yet are now forgotten. I know pastors' wives who have been pushed to the side as soon as their husbands died.

One day, as I ministered during a service, the Spirit of God led me to pray for a certain woman in the congregation. Though she had been saved for many years, the devil tormented her through the spirit of unforgiveness and bitterness. As I shared the love of God with her, she began to cry and was willing to die to these two foul spirits. In a very short time, this lady rose to levels in her relationships and life that she had been struggling to reach. Her testimony was a sure indication that God had accepted her sacrifice that day.

Motivational speakers often say that the greatest enemy to your success is yourself. I concur and add that you are the greatest prophet over your own life. The things we believe we can do, we do. We speak to ourselves and make sure we have followed our words through to see them come to pass. If we want to enjoy service to God, then we must decide to kill whatever it is that keeps drawing us back when we want to move forward. Perhaps we will have to kill some of our relationships for God to use us. There are indeed very many things God wants us to die to.

A SACRIFICE MUST BE BURNT

A sacrifice is incomplete until it is burnt. Choosing a good animal to offer and placing it on the altar does not amount to a sacrifice. That is only a carcass on an altar. God is never interested in Half-done projects. Any time you serve God, He expects you to go all the way and finish your job. God never talks of fair or not so fair. He will either commend us as good and faithful servants or see us as unfaithful servants. A sacrifice, therefore, must be burnt at the altar for God to accept it.

'Then Noah built an altar to the Lord and, taking some of the clean animals and clean birds, he sacrificed burnt offerings on it. Then God smelled the pleasing aroma and said in his heart: "Never again will I curse the ground because of man, even though every inclination of his heart is evil from childhood. And never again will I destroy all living creatures, as I have done"' (Genesis 8:20-21, NIV).

We can see that it was after God had smelled the pleasing aroma from the burning sacrifice that He made a vow. Elijah, after slaughtering the bulls and placing them on the altar didn't go away until the sacrifice was consumed by fire. He knew that it was not complete and that God had not accepted it until it was burnt. He called on God to bring down the fire. Probably, you have done many things and don't get the results you expected. Maybe your sacrifice is chosen and dead but not yet consumed by the fire.

'I baptise you in water for repentance. But after me will come one who is more powerful than I, whose sandals I am not fit to carry. He will baptise you with the Holy Spirit and with fire' (Matthew 3:11, NIV).

John the Baptist was saying that his work was to choose and prepare the sacrifice, but there was one coming with fire to burn it. To be a sacrifice acceptable to God, the fire of God must burn us. The Holy Spirit is our fire; when He burns in us, we become an acceptable sacrifice to God.

In my gap year, after completing my O-level exams, I tried my hand in farming. The starting point was clearing the shrubs on an acre of land. I had the idea to save time and effort by burning all the bushes and shrubs. I thought that by clearing the shrubs near the boundary, I would prevent the fire from crossing over to my neighbour's land. In the beginning, things were working well, but as time went by, the fire grew bigger and bigger. It started moving so fast that I became alarmed but could do nothing about it. In no time, the whole place had burnt, and worse still, the fire had crossed the boundary to my neighbour's land.

I shouted for help and many people came, but we were over-powered by the fire. A forest that would have taken years to clear was gone in less than an hour. Fire is a powerful force!

This experience can be compared to the day of Pentecost, when the Spirit of God came down in a similar manner upon the saints—with power and cleansing effects. They spoke in different tongues and prophesied and the kingdom was transformed dramatically that day. When servants are full of the Holy Spirit, they are able to achieve more for God in a short time. How one sermon brought over 3000 people to the kingdom of God can only be credited to the Holy Spirit (Acts 2).

In our lives too, there are bushes and shrubs that could take us years to clear. I battled with anger and bitterness even after receiving salvation. I would seek to resist the temptation to fight and would kneel for hours in repentance. This was a bush in my life; no amount of discipline could get me out of it. But one day, the fire of God came upon me and burnt away all my bitterness and anger. Unlike an ordinary fire, the Spirit's fire is very selective; it only burns the unwanted, leaving what is desirable. Love, forgiveness, kindness, and longsuffering were not consumed by this fire; instead they were hardened and strengthened.

Apostle Peter did a lot to and for his master, Jesus. He even cut off someone's ear in Jesus' defence. But when challenged by a girl in the courtyard of the high priest, he denied any association with Jesus. When he realised he had gone against his promise not to forsake Jesus, Peter wept bitterly. Peter was willing to die for the Lord. Though he had been chosen by Jesus to serve with Him, something was missing, the fire of the Holy Spirit. We can determine to do many things for God, but unless we have the power of the Spirit, we will not go far. Although Peter denied Jesus, once he received the power of the Holy Spirit, he achieved great things for God. He spoke in power and burned in the Holy Spirit until God accepted his sacrifice, turning over three thousand people to the kingdom of God in a single meeting. Have you tried sacrificing but failed? You can find success if you will allow the Holy Spirit to control your life.

A SACRIFICE MUST BE GUARDED

> *Then birds of prey came down on the carcasses, but Abram drove them away. As the sun was setting, Abram fell into a deep sleep* (Genesis 15:11).

We are called to be living sacrifices to God (Romans 12:1). Let us go all the way. Do not stop until the Lord has accepted us as living sacrifices. God had asked Abraham to sacrifice to Him. He prepared the sacrifice according to the Lord's specifications. He could have left it there and assumed that his work was complete. But Abraham didn't leave the altar until God had consumed the sacrifice. There are many vultures (things) that fly around your altar ready to steal your sacrifice. Do not leave your altar until God has consumed the sacrifice.

Leaving your sacrifice before God has consumed it is like a woman who carries a baby for nine months in her womb, gives birth and leaves the baby behind a bush, then goes to her husband and friends and elatedly tells them it is a bouncing baby boy or girl. There can be no joy until the people see the baby. Our joy will be complete when God has consumed our sacrifices. Do not labour to select, kill, and burn your sacrifice, only to leave it to the vultures. Guard it. Do not leave the altar. If God delays, do not give up, sleep at the altar. If your left hand gets tired use your right, but make sure you have kept the vultures off. Sacrifices are never offered in a hurry. God is the determinant. He may come immediately or may delay but He will certainly come at the right time. If you intend to be a sacrifice, holy and acceptable to the Lord, then you must guard yourself from contamination. *Above all else, guard your heart, for it is the wellspring of life* (Proverbs 4:23). There are many things that can contaminate us and make us unholy and unacceptable before God.

Contamination may come from within or outside an individual. I asked some students, 'If I took clean water, put it in a clean glass, then covered it for one year, would you consume it?' The class said an emphatic no, explaining the water would be stagnant and thus not safe for human consumption. Contamination builds from the inside when you do not allow the Spirit of God to work in you. A Christian who has refused to grow has accepted to die. What you see, hear, or do and the people you spend time with can contaminate your life.

Although God is in-charge of our lives, we have a personal responsibility to guard ourselves. God expects us to be responsible with our lives. The Bible tells us to work out our salvation with fear and trembling (Philippians 2:12). This means we have a part to play in guarding ourselves and keeping ourselves pure and holy as living sacrifices. We guard ourselves when we:

Choose good company

The company one keeps contributes a lot to their character. This is why it is said, show me your friends and I will tell you your character. If you keep good company, you will have guarded your life from evil. The people you spend time with will either affect you positively or negatively. Psalm 1 tells of the benefits of keeping good company. Choose people who value living a holy life, that is, those who are willing to let God use them; people who are willing to sacrifice for others and willing to lay aside their achievements for what lies ahead of them. Keeping good company also means having individuals who can challenge you to break the status quo. We must pursue and build strong relationships that contribute towards making us servant leaders.

Are renewed by the Spirit of God

> ... but be ye transformed by the renewing of your mind
> (Romans 12:2)

I have often wondered why a sealed mineral water bottle should have an expiry date. Where would contamination come from, yet the manufacturers seal the bottle? Lack of air circulation in stagnant water causes decay. Just as the circulation of air keeps water fresh and pure, so does the Spirit keep a Christian free from contamination. This means, we should not dwell in the old anointing, service, or prayer. We ought to go for the renewal of our minds by the Spirit through consistent Bible study and prayer.

Obey the Word of God

The Word of God will always keep us on our toes. It will challenge us every day. If you read it with openness and purity of heart, it will challenge areas of your life. Do not suppress the challenge; obey. Remember, the Word of God is sharper than any double-edged sword (Hebrews 4:12), meaning it can do more than one thing.

Don't stay at the border

A story is told of a man who was looking to hire a driver. After interviewing several applicants, he narrowed down his candidates to two. He then asked each candidate this question: 'How good are you when driving along the edge of a cliff?' One answered, 'I am such a good driver, I will drive you on the edge of the cliff and nothing will happen.' The other driver said, 'I am such a good driver, I will drive you far away from the cliff.' The latter got the job. The lesson here is to keep as far as possible from the border. Anything can happen even to the most experienced, the most anointed, or the most diligent of us. Lot stayed at the border of Sodom (Genesis 13:12). He saw the evils in that land. His daughters were equally watching and, when put in a difficult situation, ended up sleeping with their father. Never lie to yourself that you can see evil and not practice it. The images you see with your eyes are interpreted in your mind. It does not end in the retina or pupil. Choose to be inside the things of God. The border between good and evil is a dangerous place for a Christian to live in. Make a vow like Job when he said, 'I made a covenant with my eyes not to look lustfully at a woman' (Job 31:1). Stay far away from what can cause you to fall from the grace of God.

Are a people of prayer

God expects us to pray and ask Him to fill us with the Holy Spirit. Jesus taught us to ask and it will be given to us. God responds when we ask because he is a good Father. Desiring something does not bring it. I know that there are many men who desire a good marriage, but they are not even in a bad one because they have never been bold enough to propose and ask a woman to marry them. When we pray, we must ask the Lord to fill us with the Holy

Spirit. Remember He is gentle and doesn't force himself into people. 'Behold, I stand at the door and knock. If anyone hears my voice and opens the door, I will come in and dine with him, and he with me' (Revelation 3:20). God is happy when we pray. He says when we call unto Him He will answer.

> **Reflection**
>
> a. Highlight at least three things you have discovered about the call of service.
>
> b. What will you resolve to do differently based on this discovery?

CHAPTER TWO

QUALITIES OF A SERVANT

I received an invitation to speak at an international conference where I got to interact with other servants of God from different nations. One pastor loved my ministry so much that he invited me to speak in his country. This pastor was soft-spoken, relatively slow in speech, and even walked at a snail's pace. By his look and mannerism, I assumed his congregation would be small and boring, but since I had given my word, I honoured his invitation. When I landed, I was surprised to find that the man had a huge following and vibrant ministry. Prominent people in that city were members of the church. During one tea break, I decided to ask members and leaders at random this question: 'What brought you to this church and what makes you stay?' One by one, each person said they came to the church because their pastor was humble, preached slowly, and did not shout. What I thought were the pastor's weaknesses were the very things that drew people to his church.

THE QUALITIES OF A SERVANT

Just like you know a tree by its fruit, certain qualities identify individuals as sacrificial servants. They are sacrificial servants not because they have prayed for these qualities, but they work on, live by, and have tested and proven them. Remember, many people serve, but very few are serving sacrificially. In many non-church settings, I have often had someone come up to me and ask if I am a pastor. A sacrificial servant never says I am a sacrificial servant, but they exude certain characteristics that identify them even when they are not saying it out loud. These characteristics are outlined below.

PATIENCE

The Complete Christian dictionary defines patience as the ability to bear long, waiting calmly and without complaining. We cannot serve God without serving His people. To serve, patience is a necessary virtue. Impatient servants cannot serve effectively. I worked with individuals who, when they joined me in ministry, had no courage to stand before a crowd, no fashion sense, and others too young to have responsibilities entrusted to them. These same people today have become assets in my ministry. I employed patience as I allowed them to make mistakes and seek correction. Today, I have entrusted specific responsibilities to them, they complement my ministry and with confidence I can rest and expect results, because I risked patience to see them grow. It is worth noting that both the servant and those being served need patience. My leadership journey has grown because others exercised patience on me too.

A servant leader should remember that the people he or she leads or serves are not a finished product, but a work in progress. It is expected of every servant leader to give their followers a chance to grow. Apostle Paul, reflecting on the doing of God in his life and that of others said, '…Think of what you were when you were called. Not many of you were wise by human standards, not many were influential…' (1 Corinthians 1:26). In other words, Paul is saying that by the help of God and His patience, he has become who he is.

The things of God are for those who have patience. In our own eyes it may seem as if God is slow, but He expects us to be patient. God told Habakkuk to write down the vision and wait for it to come to pass. Patience is part of the fruit of the Spirit. A person without patience cannot be a servant. In 2 Timothy 2:6, apostle Paul says, 'The hardworking farmer should be the first to receive a share of the crops.' Paul is telling Timothy that a farmer must have patience to enjoy the labour of his or her hands. Nobody plants and expects a harvest the same day. Some crops take months and others years to mature. Those of us who farm have learnt that we have to prepare our land and plant our seeds long before the clouds form in the sky. After planting, we go home and wait patiently for the rain to come. Even when we do not get the rain, we do not give up but keep waiting. As a farmer waits month after month for his crops to grow and bear fruit, so should a true servant continue serving faithfully until God's appointed and perfect time.

Consistency

After years of service in my local church, God made it clear that it was time for me to serve Him as a pastor. I served my church as a manual worker and cleaner; people sometimes referred to me as a frustrated caretaker who was not paid a penny for his labour. Even though I knew with certainty God's call for me was pastoral work, I did not know how to begin. I could not go out seeking a pastoral job. Just as David never went to the palace after Samuel anointed him, God took me to my wilderness. God placed me under His servant, another pastor. I served him in different capacities. I cleaned his car, ironed his clothes, and interceded for him.

At one point his church experienced a split and many people left. I almost left too, but God instilled in me the urge to stay. This was a very expensive time for me. I served without recognition or dignity, but thanks to God, I did it for the name of Jesus. I often made this prayer: 'God almighty, I have agreed to submit under your will and plan. I will serve your servant and his church faithfully. Credit all my services to my account in heaven. When the day comes for me to begin the work you have called me to do, I will be able to withdraw from this account. Amen.'

This is a prayer many servants ought to pray as they serve.

God is not like people who will use and bruise you when you put your trust in them. Instead, He blesses you for your faithfulness. God desires stable Christians who will represent Him here on earth. If you are serving under somebody, make sure you are doing your best. Do not rebel in the name of independence. Remember, accountability is key for any leader; you will always be under some kind of leadership. Before God lifts you, He will put you in a servant's role, but your service will be credited to your account.

Years later, God spoke to the man I was serving, telling him to leave the church under my care as he went to plant another church. I could not believe my ears. Apart from being young, I was also single. To make it clear to the congregation that God had spoken to him, the pastor called me forward during a Sunday service and explained to the church what God had said, after which he prayed for me. A week later, he put everything in writing, introduced me to the church board as the new senior pastor, and handed over all the legal documents pertaining to the church. This was the doing of the Lord. The end of the story is sweet, but it took patience for the vision to come to pass.

BOLDNESS

As Moses handed the leadership baton to Joshua, he repeatedly said these words, 'Be strong and of good courage' (Deuteronomy 31:7). He was imploring Joshua to be bold. As we serve God we will encounter lots of challenges. To remain on the course of servanthood you will have to be bold. Sometimes the Lord will speak difficult things and expect you to share with the church or particular individuals. You will go through times of testing, and He expects you to remain steadfast and unwavering.

I marvel whenever I read the story of the four Hebrew brothers—Daniel, Meshach, Shadrach, and Abednego—who despite their age were as bold as lions. They challenged the king and the law. They refused to break God's commandments. They knew that there was no other God to be worshiped but Jehovah. Their choice to stick with God was a step of boldness. The apostles prayed that they might be filled with boldness to speak God's word (Acts 4:29). Servants need to pray and exercise boldness in their service. Do not suppress God's Word, however difficult to hear it may be. Do not think of the consequences of speaking what God has told you, rather, be bold and speak, and let God fight to keep His word.

Kayole, a low-income area in Nairobi, is known as a difficult place to do ministry. As one who knows first-hand about working in this area, I can tell you we have dealt with thugs, robbers, witches, drug addicts, prostitutes, etc. in the course of our ministry. There were times we would go for evening prayers with machetes. As we knelt in prayer we had them next to us. I cannot count the times we have rescued women from near-rape incidences or people being robbed outside our church. Many pastors have started churches in our area, but few have been bold enough to handle the pressure.

One time, we had set the stage ready for a crusade when a gang comprising young men well known in the area came up to us as we began the session. They gave us three options: we stop preaching with immediate effect, pay them in cash or face their wrath. One of my mentees courageously spoke out, 'We do not need your permission to preach and we will not pay.' We began to preach as they watched. They kept coming back, evening after evening, and on the last day of the crusade, one gave his life to Jesus, hallelujah!

Another time, the Lord sent me to speak with a certain man and tell him to shun evil and start serving in holiness, for God is holy. I didn't know how to communicate this to him. I took time in prayer asking God to send someone else. Instead of God sending someone else, He put more words in my heart for this man. I felt like Jeremiah when he said, '...But His word was in my heart like a burning fire shut up in my bones' (Jeremiah 20:9). I was really moved to speak it. I boldly told him what the Lord had told me. He became angry and arrogant. He started spreading malicious rumours about me. Again, the Lord told me to go back to him and give him the last warning. I didn't like the mission but I had to obey. I was labelled a 'prophet of doom and a holier than thou brother.' With no one to turn to, I turned to God in prayer with so many questions.

Two weeks later, a message came that the young man was in the hospital and he desperately wanted to see me. Although I was leaving town for a mission that day, I decided to go to the hospital first. Immediately he saw me, tears rolled down his face and he said, 'Patrick, I am sorry I never obeyed the word of God. I hardened my heart and ignored God's counsel. Please pray for my healing and I will go back and serve God. I could not hold back my tears. As I prayed, the Spirit of God told me that the man would surely die, but I was grateful that he had turned back to God.

When God gives a difficult message for someone, you might feel discouraged, guilty, or sorry after speaking it. I encourage you to relax and wait for God to act. His word is true and returns not without accomplishing its mission or purpose. Some of us have been wounded in the course of serving but this should never be a reason to give up. Choose boldness and be a faithful servant. David brought hope and victory to the Israelites when he killed Goliath. Be bold!

HOLINESS

Holiness is a state of being pure and upright in character. Since our service is to a God who is holy, we are called to holiness. The Bible tells us we are to be holy, for God is holy (1 Peter 1:16). We cannot serve a holy God if we ourselves are not holy. The only way this is achievable is by allowing the Holy Spirit to do His transforming work within us. Many believers are of the opinion that we become holy by doing some things and not doing others. This thinking is unscriptural because any works that we do in the flesh are as filthy rags in the sight of the Holy God. God says that He is the one who sanctifies us *that I might be a minister of Jesus Christ... sanctified by the Holy Spirit* (Romans 15:16). It has nothing to do with us, we only have to be obedient and allow Him to do this changing work within us. This calls for us to repent, turn around, and receive our freedom in Jesus' name. A true servant of God desires to be holy as God is holy.

FLEXIBILITY

God likes to work with servants who are flexible. It is after we set ourselves apart that we are able to fit into God's plan. Flexible people are willing to learn new ways of doing things to the glory of God. Once during a prayer meeting, I prayed for a lady to receive deliverance from evil spirits, but there was strong resistance from Satan. Then I felt the Lord lead me to do an unusual thing. I prayed over a glass of water that it might symbolise the blood of Jesus. After she took it, the lady was completely delivered. Of course, this did not go without criticism. Many theologians would agree what I did is not written in the Bible. I almost succumbed to pressure that I had done wrong, but I remembered that I acted in obedience to the Holy Spirit's leading. Responding to one of my critics, I asked whether he believes and accepts everything in the Bible. He answered in the affirmative. I then asked, 'Suppose I found your wife sick in bed, and proceeded to place my head next to hers, mouth to mouth, nose to nose as I prayed for her, would you allow it and say amen to my prayer?' The man quickly answered, 'Never! Over my dead body.' I asked him why he would not allow prayer offered in this way yet Elisha prayed in this manner and left without a word being raised against him? My friend was not willing to be flexible towards the Holy Spirit's workings. Many of the things God wants to do through us, and to us, are new and no eye has yet seen. It will take separation for you to agree to do new things as the Holy Spirit prompts you. This does not, in any way, give license for fanaticism. I am only saying that separation will bring flexibility. My pastor always told me to plan in pencil. This was his way of encouraging me to be flexible. Jonah told the Ninevites that after 40 days God would destroy them. God relented after they repented. Jonah could not believe it. He never understood why God had given him the message for the Ninevites if He already knew He would not follow through. Jonah was not being flexible at this point.

Vision (Ability to see)

There are many things that you will never enjoy until you accept the call to be separate. Though God had promised Abraham great things when He called him, they were all pegged to his obedience and to the call to separate; his ability to see awaited the separation. After Lot and Abraham separated, God spoke to Abraham.

> *The Lord said to Abram after Lot had parted from them, 'lift your eyes from where you are and look north and south, east and west. All the land you see I*

> *will give to you and your offspring forever. I will make your offspring as the dust of the earth, so that if anyone could count the dust, then your offspring could not be counted. Go walk through the length and breadth of the land, for I am giving to you'* (Genesis 13:14-17).

There is a land that God has in store for you, but you cannot see it. God told Joshua that He had given him the city of Jericho even though Jericho at the time was shut against the Israelites. From where God sits, Jericho was just a small problem to solve, but from Joshua's perspective, it was a city with walls and impossible to conquer. Joshua needed to look at Jericho from God's perspective. Servants cannot serve God effectively without aligning their perspective to God's. Many people struggle to make ends meet. They get into wrong partnerships and investments, only to end up in losing the little they have. If you keep the wrong company, you will always get your perspective wrong. God will watch you struggle with your 'Lot' until the day you say 'enough is enough'. I believe it is no coincidence that the day Abraham parted ways with Lot is the time God helped him to see the land of his inheritance.

> *The Lord said to Abram after Lot had parted from them, 'lift your eyes from where you are and look north and south, east and west. All the land you see I will give to you and your offspring forever'* (Genesis 13:14-15).

God was waiting for the moment when Abraham would separate. Wrong association will always deny you your blessing (Psalm 1). Are there people in your life making it hard for you to see the vision clearly? Identify them and then purpose to separate yourself from them. Some relationships will always keep you in a comfort zone. Comfort zones never expose you to challenges, for you have no place to build your faith.

When I moved from my rural home to the city of Nairobi, I stayed with my elder brother. Rent, food, transport, and clothing were all provided for me. Things were good and life was comfortable. The fact is, I was extremely comfortable with everything provided for me, but I owned nothing, including my bed and beddings. I began to trust God for my own house and my own things. I told my brother it was time to move out and live on my own. His question to me, 'How will you pay your rent, college fees, transport, food, and other expenses?' After some deep thought, I said, 'Well, God will provide.' He never questioned me beyond that.

I looked around and found a one-roomed house to rent. I moved in with my clothes and the few items I had. Many of my friends thought I was crazy, but I was exercising my faith in God. By faith I promised the landlord I would pay the rent. I didn't have a job and so I didn't have money, but God provided miraculously; a friend I had not seen for a long time called and blessed me with cash. It was enough to pay the deposit and a month's rent. This was the beginning of a journey of faith for me.

I thank my brother for allowing me to move out in order to learn how to use my wings, and I thank God for keeping His promise to me—to never leave or forsake me. Are you in a comfort zone and are you worried about what to do? As God leads you, step out in faith. People who perpetually stay in their comfort zones have no testimony to share. When the disciples saw Jesus walking on the water they were afraid, for they thought it was a ghost. When they learnt that it was Jesus, Peter said, 'Lord, if it is You, command me to come to You on the water' (Matthew 14:28).

They (disciples) were in a comfort zone (boat), but Peter decided to step out. Although he began to sink, the truth remains he walked on water. Perhaps the other disciples may have laughed at him, yet he had an experience they never had—walking on water. I challenge you to take hold of your faith and dare to come out of your comfort zone. Stop worrying about what may happen to you, Jesus will hold you up in case you begin to sink. Do it now!

> **Reflection**
>
> a. Of the six qualities articulated above, which one do you resonate with the most?
>
> b. Identify practical ways your ministry would be improved by applying any of these qualities.

CHAPTER THREE

SERVANTS' ATTITUDE

You must have the same attitude that Christ Jesus had.

Though he was God,[a]
he did not think of equality with God
as something to cling to.

Instead, he gave up his divine privileges[b];
he took the humble position of a slave[c]
and was born as a human being.
When he appeared in human form,[d]

he humbled himself in obedience to God
and died a criminal's death on a cross.

Philippians 2:5-8 (NLT)

I define sacrificial servanthood as serving like a servant and not like a master. John Maxwell says that everything rises and falls on leadership. I say that everything rises on sacrificial servanthood. Jesus, the Son of God was a servant to the people. 'For even the Son of Man did not come to be served, but to serve, and to give His life a ransom for many' (Mark 10:45). We have many leaders in government and private sector alike, but we lack sacrificial-servant leaders.

When the disciples wanted Jesus to tell them who their leader would be in His absence, He did not play into their mentality. Knowing very well the conventional parameters of choosing a leader like it was in the time of Saul: young, tall and handsome (1 Kings 9:3), Jesus went the opposite direction of their expectation. 'Whoever wants to become great among you must be your servant, and whoever wants to be first must be your slave—just as the Son of Man did not come to be served, but to serve, and to give his life as a ransom for many' (Matthew 20:26–28).

Many leaders can trace their fall at the point they stopped serving people, while others will trace their rising to the point at which they started serving people. Jesus was such a servant leader that even those who never believed in Him admired his leadership. So much so that Mahatma Gandhi once felt like Christians were letting Jesus down. When the missionary Eli Stanley Jones in an interview asked, 'Mr Gandhi, though you quote the words of Christ often, why is that you appear to so adamantly reject becoming his follower?' Gandhi replied, 'Oh, I don't reject Christ. I love Christ. It's just that so many of you Christians are so unlike Christ.'

When Rehoboam succeeded his father Solomon as the king of Israel. He asked for advice on how to rule his people. The elders said, 'Your father put a heavy yoke on us, but now lighten the harsh labour and the heavy yoke he put on us, and we will serve you (2 Chronicles 10:5ff). They were asking him to be a servant leader. Unfortunately, Rehoboam never followed the elders' advice; instead, he followed the advice of his fellow youth, who told him to make things harder for the people more than his father had done. Rehoboam lost his kingdom through a rebellion that followed soon after. To be a servant, one must forsake some pleasures and ranks, take a lowly place, and go to where the people who need service are. My lecturer in Bible school often said to us, 'When you go out there, feed the sheep, not the giraffes. In other words, come down to the level of your people'.

Jesus forsook the heavenly pleasures and glory to come to earth. 'Who, being in very nature God, did not consider equality with God something to be used to his own advantage; rather, he made himself nothing by taking the very nature of a servant, being made in human likeness. And being found in appearance as a man, he humbled himself by becoming obedient to death—even death on a cross! (Philippians 2:6). This was indeed a great sacrifice.

For a sacrificial servant, the attitude is that of unworthiness.

> *So, you also, when you have done everything you were told to do, should say, 'We are unworthy servants; we have only done our duty'* (Luke 17:10).

This is a principle we don't usually like to apply in our daily lives. Very few of us want to be 'unworthy servants'. Throughout our lives, we have probably met people and had experiences that have spoken to us about how worthy we are. Many consider themselves worthy because they surround themselves with power and because of the vehicles they drive, the churches they pastor, the countries they have visited, the degrees they have. The list is endless. But the challenge we face is this: if what we have or what we are working to have does not make us better servants of Christ, then we must do away with it. It is risky to count ourselves worthy. No matter the position we hold, we have been called to serve. Our service should be seen and felt by both our seniors and juniors.

Jesus Christ, our model, made it clear to us that His mission was to do the will of the Father. He served His disciples as well as the social rejects of the time. Lepers were not allowed to mix with other people. That is why the three lepers in 2 Kings chapter 7 were torn between going into a city where they were unwanted or to the enemies' camp. Jesus did not follow the world's patterns of rejection. He healed them. Unlike the Pharisees, Jesus mixed with sinners and dined with them regardless of His status. Although He was almighty God, during His time in human form, Jesus chose to set aside His rights to special privileges and acted as a humble servant rather than seeking to be served—to the point of dying for you and me.

In the Christian life today, there are too many armchair-generals who are doing little or nothing. It is time we set aside our achievements to serve God in simplicity. If we count our achievements as worthless and strive for what is ahead of us in Christ, we shall maintain our servanthood. Those who serve while considering themselves 'worthy' of special attention or status know that after all is said and done they will get some pay. Those who merely serve for what they will earn are 'worthy' servants. They are 'worthy' of what they earn in terms of salary. They watch the clock and know what time to start and when to end. I want to be a true 'unworthy' servant.

When you have an experience with a 'worthy' servant it may end up being memorable but not positive. One day I had a tooth that needed to be extracted so I booked an appointment with a dentist. I had no idea that most of my teeth were damaged and so I expected him to just pull out the aching tooth and then I would be out of pain and on my way. After the doctor extracted the tooth, he put a filling in another. He also realised there was another tooth with a cavity that was worse than the one he had already filled. He began to drill on the tooth and mid way through asked me to pay for his services. I was not prepared for the cost of repairing three teeth. My money was not enough to cover the already incurred cost. Though I was still writhing with pain from the drilled, but unfilled tooth, the dentist refused to alleviate my pain by filling it. He told me, 'My friend, I have done what your money could afford, go and come back with the balance to enable me repair the remaining tooth.'

I could not believe my ears. You can imagine me going home with an unfinished dental issue. This man considered himself a 'worthy' servant. He had clearly defined where his service would start and where it would stop.

Look around today and you will realise that 'worthy' servants are everywhere. In another instance, a brother visited our church. He was broke and needed money. He approached the office and said that God had convicted him to paint the church. We were indeed glad to hear such good news. He came the following day with half a litre of paint and painted a very small portion. When I inquired as to when he would finish his painting job, he replied, 'I was only convicted to do that portion. If you need the wall completed, we will have to negotiate a price.' It was not in our church budget at that particular time to paint the church. But the look of the small portion he had painted made the rest of the building seem very unsightly, so we had to struggle to raise funds to get the entire building repainted. This was another servant who was 'worthy' in his own eyes, but his commitment to service was extremely limited.

Godly service is a blessing to a servant who is aware of his or her unworthiness. A 'worthy' servant waits for payment from people, but an 'unworthy' servant counts on payment from heaven. A 'worthy' servant is like a hired shepherd, who will never sacrifice for the flock. When danger comes, this shepherd runs away, leaving the flock to die in the jaws of the attacking wolves and lions. A servant who does not consider him or herself to be worthy of special consideration and honour is ready to sacrifice for the flock.

THE SERVANT'S LANGUAGE

Every servant or would-be servant must speak the servant's language. It is impressive to observe people who stick to service, whether others recognise and offer accolades to them or not. Of course, there are constraints in our service to God and it would be a lie to say that being a servant is easy. Servanthood demands humility, perseverance, and consistency. In order to be successful, we must speak the servant's language. Many start off well but drop off along the way. I know a man who served God as a pastor for many years. When things began to go wrong in ministry and he saw that there was no more money coming in, he dropped his call and decided to be a bus conductor. Whenever I meet him, I always wonder to myself whether he really did receive a call to ministry. And if he did, what will he tell God when He asks for an account? Our service to God is not without ups and downs, but because we are living sacrifices, chosen and set apart, dead and burnt, we can walk against any tide or current. One of the things that will keep us moving in the face of difficulty is applying the servant's language. These words should often proceed from the mouth of a servant:

'I am an unworthy servant; I have only done my duty.'

> *So you also, when you have done everything you were told to do, should say, 'We are unworthy servants; we have only done our duty'* (Luke 17:10, NIV).

When we have served and the people we serve are happy, we can give the glory to our Master. The language of 'unworthiness' will keep us on our toes to avoid pride. Every servant must learn to use this language. Servants are always under some authority. If you never submit to the authority that God has placed over you, then you do not fit in servanthood. A pastor had served under his senior pastor for nearly two decades. He excelled in preaching and administration, perhaps even much more than his senior pastor. People approached him and told him that they were convinced that the time had come to begin his own ministry. When he prayed for God's direction, audibly the Lord told him that he should humble himself and continue to serve his senior pastor. As he did so, he saw the gifts of the Spirit flowing in his life. One time after ministering in a crusade, many people got saved and others healed. Everyone wanted to shake his hand or give him a thumbs up. To some people this might have seemed like the moment to split the church, but this man of God kept repeating these words, 'Glory to God, I am just an unworthy servant'.

In ourselves, we have nothing to make us feel worthy before God. Apostle Paul said that anything he achieved was 'by the grace of God'. This language works when things are good and when they are bad. As I pray for people to receive healing, I am quick to praise God, adding that I am just an unworthy servant. Sometimes after prayers for healing, believers die instead of getting well. Because it is God's work, not mine; I don't carry guilt or bad feelings. I am merely an obedient, 'unworthy' servant. When miracles happen as I preach or pray for the people, I praise God, for it is still His doing.

'I heard God!'

> *Then God said, 'Take your son, your only son, Isaac, whom you love, and go to the region of Moriah, sacrifice him there as a burnt offering on one of the mountains I will tell you about'* (Genesis 22:2).

When God spoke to Abraham He was very specific. He had a specific place in mind for him to go to make the sacrifice. When Abraham got to the region of Moriah he had to wait for God's direction. He needed to hear from God about the exact mountain. The reason behind this is the lamb was not on just any mountain, but in one specific place. If Abraham would have gone to a mountain of his choice he could have ended up killing his son while God never intended for this to happen. Many people are in a hurry to sacrifice before they discern which mountain God is calling them to. The provision of resources is on a specific mountain. That is where the lamb is tied. For you to get it right, you must be ready to speak the servant's language. Say, 'Yes, Lord', then follow His formula, not yours. His formula may call us to wait for further instructions at strategic points along our journey. Abraham received instructions to go to the region of Moriah and then to wait for the next set of instructions before continuing with the sacrifice. He moved forward with what was clear and when he was where God had told him to go, God gave Abraham the next set of instructions. We don't need to sit still waiting for the complete picture, we move forward with the instructions God gives us and trust that along the way, He will continue to direct and guide us. After all, it is His work, not ours. He is the author and knows each step along the way that will bring glory to Him.

I enjoyed learning math in primary school. When we were taught how to find the area of a triangle, I assumed this formula (Area = 1/2 x base x height) would work for all the other shapes too. I quickly began to apply it wherever I saw the word 'area'. It did not matter if the question asked to find the area of a circle, square, pyramid or parallelogram, I used the formula A=1/2xbxh. I would get surprised and very annoyed to get the wrong answer each time it wasn't a triangle. A correct formula applied in the wrong setting will always produce wrong results. The important lesson here is to hear from God and get the specific details before you act on your 'Yes, Lord'. Resources for service are waiting on the mountain of the Lord. As long as you have discerned the direction of God then keep going. You will not lack.

'I will not dismiss an opportunity'

> .... *And the wise heart will know the proper time and procedure* (Ecclesiastes 8:5, NIV).

Many servants have ended up being frustrated in their ministries because of their dependence on manna. Manna was survival food given to Israelites in the wilderness. God supplied the Israelites with manna until they got into the Promised Land. 'Then the manna ceased on the day after they had eaten the produce of the land; and the children of Israel no longer had manna, but they ate the food of the land of Canaan that year (Joshua 5:12). In the land of promise you engage in dairy farming for milk and beekeeping for honey. Servants become discouraged when they are waiting for manna to come while in the land of promise. The manna syndrome will continue to discourage, frustrate, and even kill servants. God provides his servants opportunities so they can work and eat of the produce of the land.

I have received money in the course of my service. I praise God for His provision, but I have learnt that most times, this money has come my way from opportunities I have ceased at just the right time and with God's favour upon the work of my hands. I once asked God to provide a specific amount of money I needed for a certain project that seemed so far out of reach at the time. Deep in my heart I heard a voice asking, 'What is that amount in the eyes of God?' I received comfort and continued in my service knowing that, 'in the mountain of the Lord, it shall be provided.' Some days later, I had a conversation with a gentleman who, out of the blue, asked if I could help him buy a car. I had never transacted a car deal before. Just before I could say no, I heard myself say, yes. The man was elated and immediately went ahead to pay the necessary amounts to facilitate the purchase. When I delivered the vehicle to his doorstep with all the accompanying documents, he was so excited and pleased at the efficiency and integrity I had exercised in the transaction that he paid a generous commission for my efforts. I must say that the amount I received was eight times more than the amount I had prayed for.

Opportunities are rarely labelled as such, nor do they come shouting, 'look here, we are opportunities, take us!' To servants, they are like a mountain: you see it well when you get nearer; for non-servants, they are like a mirage, which disappears as you get closer. The more you keep serving, the more you will discern the opportunities available to you. The Bible says that the kingdom of heaven is like treasure hidden in a piece of land (Matthew 13:44). Opportunities are also hidden: those who seek find them.

'It's God and me'

> *For with God nothing will be impossible* (Luke 1:37).

A servant whose trust and motivation is in God is unshakable. They believe that in God, all things are possible. This is the confidence we ought to have as servants of God. Who would stand before a king to declare a three and a half-year drought or challenge the prophets of Baal and Jezebel to call down fire from heaven, unless their trust was in God? It feels good to work for God, but it is even more satisfying when He works through us. Team up with God if you want to do exploits.

One young boy consistently prayed for his dad to buy a car. After some time, the boy thought perhaps he ought to help his father buy the car. He took all the coins he had, totalling 1 USD, and presented them to his father, telling him he could use the amount to buy the car. It so happened that the father had actually purchased the car and it was coming home the following day. You can imagine the little boy's excitement when he saw the father come home that evening driving. He ran all over the neighbourhood telling the other children how he and his father had jointly bought a brand-new car. Gideon knew this well. When he went to war, he trained his soldiers to say, "A sword… for the Lord and for Gideon"'(Judges 7:20). Trust in God and team up with Him. Work with God and let Him work through you. Trust that when you go through the fire or water, He is with you and when He has finally brought you onto a smooth place, maintain the relationship and do not forsake Him.

'No turning back'

> *No one who puts his hand to the plough and looks back is fit for service in the kingdom* (Luke 9:62).

Servants who have sacrificially given themselves to Jesus never turn back. When they go through fire they neither stop nor turn back, they keep walking. No wonder when our Lord addressed His disciples He said, 'And these signs will follow those who believe' (Mark 16:17-18). Jesus was teaching them to keep walking and not turn back. They were past the place of waiting for miracles. They were ahead. Miracles know our back. When you run after them they will run from you. They never know our faces. Do you remember how you began the race? You were not a person of any influence (1 Corinthians 1:26). By the grace of God, you have come this far. Never turn to admire anything, keep moving. You have really come too far to despair or give up now.

Reflection

a. Share how the servant's language makes you a better servant.

b. What new discoveries have you made about servanthood from this chapter?

CHAPTER FOUR

OBSTACLES TO SERVICE

> *...Watch out for those...obstacles in your way that are contrary to the teachings you learned* (Romans 16:17, NIV).

I was 27 years old when I began full-time ministry. I had prayed and fasted over it and my heart was at peace. I knew with clarity what God had called me to do. One day, I excitedly shared several things God had showed me concerning my ministry with David, a brother in the Lord. I was disappointed that David did not share my enthusiasm. Instead, he told me these words that only made sense many years later: 'Patrick, there is quite a big gap between, thus says the Lord, and it came to pass.' Many years later, some of the things God showed me are yet to manifest.

I have gone through obstacles that would have made me give up. Sometimes these obstacles never go away, but a servant must forge ahead despite them. I share a few below.

FEAR

I have been through issues that released nothing into me but fear. Whenever the devil wants to fight a Christian, he begins by instilling fear in his or her heart. Any time you find yourself at a place where fear is trying to control your life, be very careful. Fear is not from God (2 Timothy 1:7). Many battles are fought in the mind, before they happen in real life. Goliath conquered the minds of the Israelites by instilling fear in them through intimidation.

> *'And the Philistine said, 'I defy the armies of Israel this day; give me a man, that we may fight together.' When Saul and all Israel heard these words of the Philistine, they were dismayed and greatly afraid.'* (1 Samuel 17:10-11).

We do not have an account of what Goliath had done previously. We are only told of his size, his weapon, and his threats. Goliath could have used one spear and one sword at a time, just like any other soldier would. Yet through his threats and bravado he filled the Israelites with fear.

> *There is no fear in love; but perfect love casts out fear...*
> (1 John 4:18)

A story is told of a king whose nation was very corrupt and immoral. This king was troubled and prayed for help. God told the king He would help him, but that meant killing four thousand corrupt and immoral people with a plague. Since the king had no other solution, he consented. The following day, the plague hit the country and forty thousand people died. The king was very bitter towards God and asked why He had killed more people than they had agreed. God responded, 'I only killed four thousand but when the other thirty-six thousand people saw it, fear overcame them and they died.' This is the kind of power fear can have! Fear is dangerous and not from God; die to it!

Overcoming Fear

One must handle fear head-on. I used to think that I could overcome fear by ignoring it or stating that I was not afraid. This never made me courageous. Overlooking issues will never make fear go away, however, the following points will help you eradicate fear.

Knowledge of God's Word

As long as the Word of God is in one's heart, fear cannot take control. The confidence of a lawyer is in his knowledge of the law. That is why he can stand and boldly defend an accused person. He is fully aware that he cannot be jailed for defending even a murderer. The confidence of a Christian is directly proportional to his/her knowledge of the Bible. I once attended a conference where one of the facilitating pastors shared this story: the American army was deployed for a peacekeeping mission in the Amazon region. Just before departure, they were paraded before their commander for last-minute instructions. He told them where they were going had huge snakes called anacondas. Then he gave this advice: 'When you see an anaconda, do not fear and do not run; lie down and cooperate. It will begin to swallow you from your legs, and then move to your knees. At that point, do not fear and do not move. It will swallow you up to your hips, again do not fear nor move. It will swallow you up to your waist but will not go beyond, because your sword, fixed at your waist, will stop it. At that point, remove your sword from the scabbard and slice the snake into two. You will have killed the anaconda.' The commander's secret was not in the advice of don't fear, but the sword fixed at the waist. As long as servants have the Word of God, they ought not to fear. The Bible is the servant's sword.

God's Word will keep a servant moving even when a promise seems to delay. It is that word that we have treasured in our hearts that gives us strength and confidence. When the angels visited Mary and Joseph when Jesus was a baby, and told them everything God had in store for their son, The Bible says, Mary treasured up all these things and pondered them in her heart (Luke 2:19). No wonder, during the wedding in Cana of Galilee when the wine was finished, Mary asked Jesus for help telling the disciples to do whatever He would ask them to. Mary was confident that Jesus had help for the people because of the word she had received concerning Jesus when He was a child.

Hang on to the promises of God

There are many people who live under the fear of death. Others are constantly worried that their spouses or children may die. If you find yourself in such a situation then you should hold on to the promises of God:

> *I shall not die, but live, and declare the works of the Lord* (Psalm 118:17).

If you are a young parent and the devil keeps on threatening your lineage, refuse to succumb to the voice of the enemy declare with the psalmist:

> *'Yes, may you see your children's children...'* (Psalm 128:6).

Fear is a burden that only Jesus can handle. One prophet of doom prophesied to me that I would die within seven days. I took it lightly but in those seven days, I almost died in seven different occasions. Slowly, fear began to grip my heart. I was on the verge of giving up but God ministered to me through His Word. He began to tell me, 'The Lord will keep you from all harm—He will watch over your life, The Lord will watch over your coming and going both now and forever more' (Psalm 121:7-8). As these words penetrated my heart and mind, I began to see the power of God and eventually fear was driven out.

Caleb held on to the promises of God. Not even old age could stop him from receiving his promise.

> ...*Just as the Lord promised he has kept me alive for forty-five years...so here I am today, eighty-five years old! I am still as strong today as the day Moses sent me out; I am as rigorous to go out to battle now as I was then* (Joshua 14:10-11).

Live a holy Life

Another weapon that fights fear is holiness. A person who lives a holy life has nothing to fear. My primary school teacher would ask us whether we were righteous if he noted fear in us. I never understood his question until I read this Scripture, 'The wicked flee when no one pursues, but the righteous are bold as a lion' (Proverbs 28:1). A servant who has nothing that accuses him before God rarely is a victim of fear.

EXPERIENCES

Amongst the many things that we have to let go are some of our life experiences. Our life experiences shape our behaviour. Some of them were good and others bad. Good experiences are those that never take away our dependence on God. If an experience takes away our dependence on God or our obedience to His Word, it is a bad one, and one we ought to die to.

> *When Jesus had finished speaking, He said to Simon, 'Put out into deep water, and let down the nets for a catch'. Simon answered, 'Master we've worked hard all night and haven't caught anything. But because you say so, I will let down the nets'* (Luke 5:4-5, NIV).

Apostle Peter was an experienced fisherman. He could have dismissed Jesus' words and banked on his past experiences. He knew very well that fishing had to be done at night when there is no light to scare the fish away. The Lord Jesus was not a fisherman but a carpenter. What could a carpenter tell an experienced fisherman? Peter had toiled the whole night catching nothing.

Experience would have told Peter, if you do not have any luck at one place then try elsewhere. It would have been easier for Peter if Jesus had sent him to another place. Fortunately, Peter was willing to die to his past experiences. May we be willing to die to our experiences in order for us to hear and obey God's Word.

> *Not that I have already attained, or am already perfected; but I press on, that I may lay hold of that for which Christ Jesus has also laid hold of me* (Philippians 3:12).

Apostle Paul's writings have been a tremendous blessing to me. Though he had achieved a lot in God, he was always ready to forget his past success in order to see God in new ways. As long as we keep holding on to past experiences, we deny ourselves the chance of enjoying the future. If you learn to die to your experience, you will be sure to experience God in new ways. God is not a train that only follows a predetermined track. He can and will use many means to bless you. If you can hold your personal expertise and experience loosely, you will begin to enjoy your service to God.

> *He found a fresh jawbone of a donkey, reached out his hand and took it, and killed a thousand men with it. And so, it was, when he had finished speaking, that he threw the jawbone from his hand, and called that place Ramath Lehi* (Judges 15:15,17).

God used Samson in many special ways. When God's Spirit rested on him, he used a jawbone to kill a thousand men. This was a great achievement. Maybe I might not have thrown away the bone, but would have kept it for another time when enemies might strike again. Perhaps you too would have done the same, but Samson didn't make this mistake, and thus, limit God. The Bible says that he threw it away. Just because God moved mightily through a certain 'bone' doesn't mean that we must keep it. Many of us are holding on to some bones just because God used them once to do something great. Let them go! They are barring you from seeing greater things.

Although David used a sling and a stone to bring down Goliath, it is not recorded anywhere else in Scripture that he used this weapon again to win a battle. In other places we see him using a sword or a spear. He never limited God to a sling. Probably, God has taken you through good experiences where you have had success, but good may well be the enemy of best. The things that God has for you, no eye has seen, no ear has heard, and no mind has conceived (1 Corinthians 2:9). The Bible says that man shall not live by bread alone but by every word that proceeds from the mouth of God (Deuteronomy 8:3). The best way of dealing with experiences is by depending on the voice of God. Don't be a slave of a jawbone or a sling and stones. Keep on moving with Jesus. God is always on the move.

DISCOURAGEMENT

No one is immune to discouragement. Every servant is prone to it. God knew that Joshua would face discouragement, so He gave these words of wisdom.

> *No one will be able to stand against you all the days of your life. As I was with Moses, so I will be with you;*

> *I will never leave you nor forsake you. Be strong and very courageous...* (Joshua 1: 5-6).

Many people have ceased to be sacrifices to God because of discouragement. Everyone is vulnerable to attack, whether you are a pastor, king, lawyer, or housewife. A story is told of a man who had a vision. He visited the devil's workshop and noticed many powerful weapons with price tags on them. A wooden weapon displayed on the table had the highest price among many that were made of silver or gold. He turned it on one side and read the name there: 'discouragement'. When asked why it was so expensive even though it was only made of wood, the devil replied. 'It is the weapon that opens doors to the rest. If you cannot get in using any of the others in Christian warfare, use discouragement and a breakthrough will come.'

Discouragement can cause the strongest soldier to shoot himself and die. A discouraged Judas could not imagine forgiveness, so he committed suicide. A discouraged Elijah desired death even though he had achieved great triumphs for Jehovah. There are numerous cases of discouraged spouses who have ended up in divorce. There is a way out of discouragement.

It is important for you to keep in mind that Satan is a schemer. He is always looking for areas where we are most vulnerable. He looks for opportunities where he would realise the highest number of casualties if he struck. Do not give him a chance, keep yourself guarded and alert. Live every moment with Jesus and keep on walking.

> *The days are evil therefore see to it that you walk circumspectly, not as fools but as wise, redeeming the time* (Ephesians 5:15).

There are two instances the devil loves dropping discouragement to servants of God:

After victory or breakthrough

Many of God's servants are attacked immediately after a breakthrough. The objective is to confuse the mind and make one feel as if he or she made a mistake in the process of achieving the breakthrough. We begin to blame ourselves, missing a chance for praise, celebration, and thanksgiving to God. In 1 Samuel chapter 30, we read David and his soldiers had won the battle against the Philistines. As they marched to their homes with the expectation of songs and shouts of joy from their wives and children, discouragement awaited them. The enemy had struck in their absence, burning the whole village and carrying away all their property as well as their children and wives. The enemy denied them a chance to celebrate and glorify God. The soldiers blamed their leader, David.

Elijah, the man of God, had achieved breakthrough by restoring the worship and holy fear of Jehovah. Anyone would expect this to be a time for celebrating victory, but hardly had Elijah began to celebrate, when the enemy struck with discouragement (1 Kings 19). A demon-possessed Jezebel arose with threats, swearing by her gods to kill Elijah. A discouraged Elijah hid himself and began desiring death.

Just before victory

I knew a young man who was a sound engineer in a certain church. He was very committed to his work and his pastor really loved and trusted him. The pastor was always sure that this brother would be in church for every church event or meeting. The sound engineer had begun to get tired and discouraged with his work, complaining about his little pay and that no one ever noticed how hard he worked. One day, the church had a guest preacher from another country visiting. That day, the sound engineer decided to teach his pastor and the church a lesson. He put off his phone and never showed up for the meeting. As the pastor wondered what to do, a young man who used to sit near the sound desk offered to step in and try to save the situation. It so happened that the young man did such a good job that really impressed the guest preacher. After the meeting, the preacher offered to host this stand-in soundman and hone his skills further. It was the time for the sound engineer to fly out of the country and work abroad, but in his hour of breakthrough, discouragement attacked, causing him to miss his opportunity. The stand-in took his place, went abroad, got his work permit, studied there, and the rest, as they say, is history.

The most intense part of any battle is just before it is over. I will never forget an incident when I was in high school. One particular student was notorious for bullying others. I tried to ensure that our paths never crossed at any time. Unfortunately, the thing I greatly feared came to pass. The bully decided to start a fight with me. This would be one of the most humiliating and painful moments in my life as I envisioned being beaten before other students. I took the risk of challenging this bully saying whatever was bound to happen would happen. The fight didn't take more than five minutes, but it became so hot that I contemplated giving in.

Discouragement was about to overcome me. Little did I know that my opponent felt the same way. After just a few punches and kicks, the bully took off. You can imagine how relieved I felt and the cheers I received from the students. From that time, I was delivered from the wrath of this bully. I started to walk with my head high and chest out. I am glad I didn't run away when the fight was hot, for my victory was just around the corner.

When David heard of what Goliath was doing to the Israelites, he declared that he would attack and kill him. He started by speaking peace to the Israelites. In 2 Samuel 17:32, David said to Saul, 'Let no one lose heart on account of this Philistine, your servant will go and fight him.' David was set for breakthrough and prepared a solution for the discouraged army of Israel. As soon as the devil saw David's determination, courage, faith, and the breakthrough awaiting him, he entered Eliab, David's elder brother, who became very harsh towards David. David refused to be discouraged and continued with his plan, for he knew that breakthrough was around the corner.

When Saul's armour would not fit him, he refused to let it be a stumbling block. He never wished that he were a little bigger or taller; he just apologised as a matter of courtesy and moved on towards breakthrough with his sling. When your seniors despise you and kings' clothes cannot fit you, do not start to lament and wish for what you don't have. Move on with what you do have and as the person you are, for victory awaits.

Handling Discouragement

Encourage yourself in the Lord

In 1 Samuel 30:6 things are not going well for David. The city had been burnt and the children and women taken as captives. His soldiers were discouraged and were planning to stone him. Having no one to turn to, the Bible says, 'David strengthened himself in the Lord his God.'

Rarely will one find a Barnabas (son of encouragement) on every corner in life. This is why it is important to have your own source of encouragement: God. Encourage yourself and say like Job, 'For I know that my Redeemer lives' (Job 19:25). Since I went into full-time ministry relatively young, when I faced challenges I often felt overwhelmed. At some point, I had not paid my house rent, the church was involved in a legal battle with the court ruling in favour of the plaintiff, which meant we had to pay damages and legal fees, there was no money in the church, and whatever people gave as offering was too little. I had prayed and heaven seemed silent. I decided to share my problems with my bishop for I thought; perhaps he would give me some money. He sounded quite concerned and moved as I poured all my problems to him over the phone. He gave me all the time to talk just like a good counsellor. When I was done he asked, 'Are you through?' When I answered in the affirmative, he then said, 'Muriithi, I have just a few words for you, welcome to the ministry.' With those words he concluded the conversation. I was so discouraged and frustrated. Then I remembered David. Because he had no one to encourage him, he encouraged himself in the Lord, and so I did the same. I believe with all my heart that I am who I am today because I have refused to bow to discouragement. I know my bishop had nothing against me; he only wanted me to learn to exercise my faith. Today we laugh about it.

Know the Word of God

God's Word will take us through terrible times. I believe that the reason the three young Hebrew men, Shadrach, Meshach and Abednego, overcame discouragement is because they knew the Word of God well. They knew that their God did not leave nor forsake his people. Isaiah 43:1 helps us to understand that God accompanies us in every place that we go whether through fire, water, death or anything else. The Word you have in your heart will keep you strong. This was the difference between Gehazi and Elisha in 2 Kings chapter 6. Gehazi saw the enemy while Elisha saw the angels who were on their side. What you know will give you peace or fear.

Focus on Jesus and not issues

There are many issues that can keep a servant off-mark. If a servant does not train himself to maintain their focus on Jesus, his or her productivity is usually wanting. When the snakes in the wilderness bit the Israelites (Numbers 21:4-9), they prayed to God for help. God instructed Moses to make a bronze snake and put it on a pole. Anyone who looked at it was healed. It is possible, that there were many who were so bitter and mad at God and the snakes that they opted not to look at the bronze snake. Others perhaps wished that God would kill the snakes. They clung to their wishes and died. To overcome discouragement, look upon Jesus and not at the issue. I applied for my passport at a time in Kenya when the process was tedious and rife with corruption and uncooperative officers. On my first attempt, the officer in charge arrogantly chased me away from his office and for no legitimate reason. As I walked out of the building, a man I never knew approached me, smiling. He asked me why I was there, and I explained everything, including what had happened with the officer. He picked up my documents and asked me to follow him. As we walked through the corridors of the immigration office, I could read some notices on the wall. 'Non-staff will be prosecuted' I began to ask myself many questions: do I know who this man is? What if he is a conman? What if I am prosecuted? I think he read my mind and told me not to read what was on the wall otherwise I would lose my faith. In less than four hours I had a passport that would usually take several months, if not years, to get. Keep your eye on Jesus and not issues.

PRIDE

> *A man's pride will bring him low, but the humble in Spirit will retain honour* (Proverbs 29:23).

One of the worship leaders at the church was an extremely gifted singer. She was sought after to lead worship in many meetings around the country. One day, she was called upon to lead worship in a meeting where the late Reinhard Bonke would be in attendance. She told me that when she stood to sing, no sound came out of her mouth. She could not do a single song. Then God spoke to the preacher and told him that the lady was suffering because of her pride. Reinhard prayed and her voice returned, but it was not the same as her original voice. One of the ways of overcoming pride is by attributing your success or achievements to God and doing everything as a leader for God's glory. There is nothing a servant can achieve without the master's help. The truth of the matter is, a servant has nothing of his own.

Pride will always enthrone self. It is an indicator of a person who is falling. Pride comes before a fall. Not many people who are proud know that they are proud. Pride is like weight; you never know when you are gaining it. Achievements can make a person proud. This is why it is important to 'Humble yourself in the sight of the Lord, and he will lift you up' (James 4:10). I once heard someone pray asking God to humble him. I think the reason why God told us to humble ourselves is because if he did it, it can be serious. He humbled Nebuchadnezzar, Herod, Pharaoh and it did not end well. Do not wait for God to humble you, humble yourself. Pride takes God away from someone's equation of life, leadership, or achievement.

Reflection

a. Of the obstacles mentioned above. which ones have you encountered in the course of your service?

b. Identify ways you will deal with each obstacle mentioned.

CHAPTER FIVE

SERVANTS' TESTS

Dear brothers and sisters,[a] when troubles of any kind come your way, consider it an opportunity for great joy. For you know that when your faith is tested, your endurance has a chance to grow. (James 1:2-3 (NLT)).

My high school mathematics teacher once introduced a topic he knew we disliked by giving us this story. 'All through high school, I managed to get 100% in only one paper: mathematics. It had 50 questions but the instructions on the front page read, "read all the questions and answer none."' He went on to tell us how everyone in the class were busy calculating as he sat doing nothing. They probably pitied him because they thought he had nothing to write. When they were given their papers back, he was the only one who scored 100% while others scored zero. He finished his story with a lesson: if one gets the instructions right, they are likely to score more. I pray that every servant will get the instructions right. It is a warning, however, that a servant will be tested. To ascertain one has gone through their driving lessons properly, drivers are subjected to a driving test. If they pass, they receive a license, and if they fail, they repeat the test. One cannot effectively handle God's people without going through training and passing the servanthood test. In *Leadership Pitfalls*, I articulate the three preparatory schools of leadership. In this section, I share the four tests every servant goes through, derived from the temptation of Jesus (Matthew 4:1-11).

IDENTITY

> ...*'If You are the Son of God, command that these stones become bread'* (Matthew 4:3).
>
> ... *'If You are the Son of God, throw Yourself down'* (Matthew 4:6).

The first test a servant must pass is the test of identity. By implying if Jesus were the Son of God, He would turn the stones to bread or throw Himself down and the angels would bear Him up, Satan was telling Jesus to prove His identity. Satan was aware that Jesus is the Son of God, so what is the big deal in asking Him to prove it? Whoever gives you orders is your master. Jesus being the Son of God and God at the same time, could not take orders from the devil. Servants must know who their master is. A servant who takes orders from the devil has a problem with identity. Jesus handled this so well when He told the devil that it is written, 'Do not put the Lord your God the test' (Matthew 14:7). I know my identity. I am your Lord. Do not tell me what to do.

In the animal kingdom, a lion is an example of one who knows his identity. He is the 'king of the jungle.' Amazingly, he is not the biggest, nor the fastest, nor the tallest, yet he is the 'king'.

When a servant is aware of who he serves, he is never ordered around by the devil. When a servant is sure of their identity, they are not insecure in their service to God. Do God's assignment and refuse to be diverted by the devil. Keep your eyes fixed on Jesus and do His will. God is happy to have faithful and obedience servants. When the sons of Eli disobeyed God, He vowed to raise other ministers. 'I will raise up for myself a faithful priest, who will do according to what is in my heart and mind' (1 Samuel 2:35). Make your master happy by following his orders. Refuse to play into the game of the enemy.

POWER

> ...'*If You are the Son of God, command that these stones become bread*' (Matthew 4:3).

The second test is the test of power ('turn these stones into bread'). As we serve the Lord, He trust us with power. This power is never for show and must be used for God's glory. A servant has to be careful not to fall into the trap of proving how powerful he or she is or misusing the power they have. God had trusted the sons of Eli with service. They were supposed to serve people and God. Instead of being faithful and using their position to help people and to glorify God, they became evil and used their power selfishly. We must be careful not to take advantage of our position as we serve people. The rule in servanthood is, the more you rise, the more you should decrease. Position comes with power. When God gives us a position, we must use that position and power with reverence to Him.

The sons of Eli used their position to oppress people. What they did as priests then happens today too, but we mustn't forget that the God we serve is holy and He expect us to be holy. 'Now Eli, who was very old, heard about everything his sons were doing to all Israel and how they slept with the women who served at the entrance to the tent of meeting...' (1 Samuel 2:22). Power must be used to lift and not to destroy. David Kadalie in *Leaders' Resource Kit,* says that serving leadership involves an approach to power and authority that works for the best interest of others while pursuing the purposes of God.

ELEVATION

> *Again, the devil took him to a very high mountain and showed him all the kingdoms of the world and their splendour* (Matthew 4:8).

The high mountain is a place of elevation. As we serve God, he elevates us to higher levels and exposure. This high place gives us a better view of life. To one who never had a house, a car or money, when he or she gets them, it is elevation. Many people fall when they begin to get elevated. Jesus saw the wealth the devil offered, but he never went for it. I have seen believers who started life at a very low point, when a meal for a day was a testimony, but when they began to get elevated, they became arrogant.

It is possible for a servant to master your elevated status and cause it not to become a stumbling block to your acts of service. There is a congregant who faithfully comes every Monday to clean the church compound and polish my shoes. He has done this for many years. One day, a pastor friend was visiting when this congregant came to the office requesting to polish our shoes. As the man walked out with both pairs of shoes in his hands, my friend turned to me and said, 'Patrick, you are really oppressing these people. What will this man take home after polishing the shoes?' I told him that he could ask the man that question when he returned. When the man came back, my guest pulled out a KES 100 note and offered it to the man and asked if he had any prayer request. My congregant politely refused the money and I asked him to tell my guest a little about himself. He went on to say that he was a former Kenya Air Force officer and an aircraft engineer, now working as a manager for a popular airline in the city. Since Monday was his day off, he had offered to polish the pastor's shoes (military style) and clean the church compound. My friend was embarrassed, to say the least, and although he did pray for my congregant, I knew he had learnt the lesson not to judge a man by his appearance and service acts.

Though Jesus was higher than all His disciples, He lived with them and worked with them. He was so much like them that when the Romans wanted to kill Him they had to depend on Judas, Jesus' disciple, to tell them who He really was among them. I decided to cut grass in our church compound one day. As I cut the grass, a man entered the compound looking for the senior pastor. When I tried to inquire what he wanted, he refused to talk to me insisting that his matter needed the senior pastor and not juniors. Finally, he proceeded to the office. Upon inquiring and he got to know that I was the senior man he was looking for, the man was very ashamed. I have trained myself to deal with my elevation by serving even in the lowest of places without feeling degraded.

Whenever church members express a desire to serve in any department in the church, we take them through our School of Ministry (SoM) where we teach, among many other things, servanthood. One brother, as part of the SoM practical assignment, was asked to clean the toilets. He did it so well and without complaining. Later, many people were shocked to learn he was a bank manager. A servant must overcome the pride that comes with elevation.

Worship

> ... 'All these things I will give You if You will fall down and worship me' (Matthew 4:9).

The fourth test is the test of worship. The devil told Jesus He could get all the wealth He had seen if only He worshipped Satan. This test looks like the simplest of the other three. Only bowing and worshipping you ask? Worship belongs to God. God is jealous and never shares His glory or worship with men. Many servants fail when they are tested on this. They either receive worship or they give it to the wrong person. When Peter and John healed the cripple, who wanted to worship them, they were quick to refuse the worship and point to Jesus (Acts 3).

When Herod accepted worship, God struck him dead. When the devil tried to take the place of God, he lost his position. Although worship looks simple, it is never simple. A servant must watch their knees, mouth, and heart when it comes to worship. The first level is bowing. Next your mouth speaks, and then your heart covenants in worship. Do not bow to no one but God and do not sell your heart. Many people have lost their position in God because of earthly things. God will not use you and dump you. He rewards His servants. Serve Jesus, worship Him only, for your labour is not in vain.

Reflection

a. Which of these four tests are you currently struggling with?

b. What resolves have you made, based on your reading, on how you will move forward in your worship and service to God?

CHAPTER SIX

SERVANTS' REWARDS

Whatever you do, work at it with all your heart, as working for the Lord, not for human masters, since you know that you will receive an inheritance from the Lord as a reward. It is the Lord Christ you are serving. (Colossians 3:23-24 (NLT)).

Our God rewards those who diligently serve Him. In as much as we do not serve God for a reward, it is good for you to know that it is not for nothing that we serve Him. Even the devil knows that our service to God has a reward. When God asked him whether he had considered Job, God's servant, the devil asked. 'Does Job fear [serve] you for nothing? (Job 1:9). It is true that we do not serve God for nothing.

People rarely notice or talk against a servant until their rewards start coming. I have done many acts of service in the course of my ministry and service to God. From washing clothes, polishing shoes, cleaning vehicles, teaching children, etc. I know without a doubt that I have received a reward in this lifetime for my ministry to God, even though that is not why I did those acts of service. I know many naysayers who ridiculed me whenever they found me cleaning the church compound. One even sarcastically asked why I left huge farms upcountry to come to the city to clean a church compound. Others told me that as long as I followed pastors, I would amount to nothing. Another warned that the most unthankful institution to ever work for is the church. Thank God I was not working for the church; I serve God in the church.

When the rewards begin to come in, people begin to label the servants. When I didn't have even a bicycle, many were okay with me. They were willing to offer free rides in their vehicles and to feed me. When I was in tattered clothes and 'holey' shoes it was okay to them, for I remained under their mercies. When I started driving, they called me a devil worshipper. When I wore a new suit, they said I was proud. I always pity servants of God. When they have nothing, they are said to be humble. When they start to enjoy the reward of their labour, they are called devil worshippers and are accused of 'eating' God's money or oppressing their poor members. Let me encourage a pastor. If anyone accuses you of 'eating' God's money, find out whether they 'eat' Satan's money. If they say you are coning the poor, find out what happened to the rich members.

Don't be deceived; it is not for nothing that we serve God. Your labour in the Lord is not in vain; you shall surely reap a good reward. Let me share a few rewards of service.

Provision

'Who serves as a soldier at his own expense? Who plants a vineyard and does not eat of its fruit? Who tends a flock and does not drink of its milk?' (1 Corinthians 9:7). Paul had been in service but realised that the people had denied him a chance to use God's resources for God's service. A story is told of two missionaries who went to preach in a far country. They both boarded a train, but one paid more money for a comfortable coach and the other boarded the lowest class. When they arrived at their destination, the one who paid for the lowest class was too tired to preach upon arrival. The one who had paid more for comfort was eager and able. After several days of ministry, the one who was very tired asked the other, 'How were you able to preach in all the meetings despite the long journey and the tiredness?' The other man told him, 'I spent God's money to do His work. You saved His money and never did His work.'

As a young man of 19, done with high school and with time in my hands, I decided to join and serve in a new church that had opened in our neighbourhood. Since I did not have any money to purchase tangible things for the church, I offered to serve my pastor. Every Friday, I would go to his home, feed his cows and work on the farm. I served this man the best way I knew how. One day, he came home from church wearing a faded shirt with its collar worn-out. Although I did not have any money, I knew I needed to do something for my pastor. When I received my 'caution money' from my high school, I decided to use it to purchase a shirt and tie for my pastor. When I presented the package to him, he shed tears. Then he prayed for me, 'Father, how many well able people have seen my nakedness but did nothing? I know this young man is doing this out of a clean heart of service. Because of what he has done, clothe him for me. His wife and children, Father clothe them for me.' I didn't have a wife or children, at the time, but he prayed for them to be clothed. Many years later, I still enjoy the result of that prayer. I have seen people, locally and from different parts of the world, clothe my wife, children, and me. Servanthood attracts provision. The pages would not be enough for me to share how, I have received vehicles, land, a house, all because of service.

Once, on a ministry assignment in the USA, my friend and I spent time walking the streets window shopping. We came across a shop displaying very nice looking suits. I told my friend we should enter and look around. He was reluctant, saying it would be a waste of time since the suits looked well beyond our means. Anyway, he obliged me and we entered the shop. Indeed, the suits were really nice and very expensive. Since the shop attendants allowed fitting, I opted to try on a pair of shoes and a suit. Looking at myself in the mirror and pleased with my reflection, I exclaimed out loud, Hallelujah! Immediately, a man began to walk in our direction. His face revealed that he wasn't pleased, but since I knew I had done nothing wrong, I did not care. When the man got to where we were standing, he asked, 'Are you a preacher?' I responded in the affirmative, mentioning where I was from and what had brought me to the US. Then pointing at the suit he asked, 'Do you like the suit?' 'Oh yes!' I responded, to which he replied, 'Pick out another one and I will pay for both.' You can imagine my excitement. At the end of our time in that shop, I walked out with two suits, two pairs of shoes, two shirts and two ties that I did not pay for with my own money. As we chatted about the day with my friend later that evening, he said I paid 'hallelujah' dollars for my new clothes and shoes.

IMPARTATION

People are always looking for shortcuts to breakthroughs. Once, a man told me he admired the grace I carry and would want an impartation from me. He proceeded to give an offering for prayer. What a cheap, simple, and evil way of getting the gift of God. I remembered the passage in Acts 8:18-20 where Simon wanted to buy the gift of God from Peter. 'Give me this power as well,' he said, 'so that everyone on whom I lay my hands may receive the Holy Spirit.' But Peter replied, 'May your silver perish with you, because you thought you could buy the gift of God with money!' Admiration or money can never cause a transfer of the gifts of God. It is serving until you are told these words, 'I no longer call you servants, but friends' (John 15:15).

Money can never buy impartation. The best way to get impartation is through service. I do not know how it works, but I have seen it work because it is God's principle. Elisha served Elijah. He must have been a great servant. When it was time for Elijah to depart, he asked Elisha, 'Tell me, what can I do for you before I am taken away from you?' 'Please, let me inherit a double portion of your spirit,' Elisha replied. 'You have requested a difficult thing,' said Elijah. 'Nevertheless, if you see me as I am taken from you, it will be yours. But if not, then it will not be so' (2 Kings 2:9-10). Elijah acknowledged that the request was beyond human abilities. Elisha was faithful to the end and got his request. Many people who serve faithfully end up receiving their leader's spirit; that is impartation. The Bible records that the last miracle Elijah performed was the first miracle that Elisha performed, and he continued in that manner. Elisha must have been a real servant. Many people today want to serve at high tables in white garments. Elisha did even the least. When at some point the king of Israel was looking for a prophet to inquire whether they should go to battle or not, Elisha came in the picture, described not as a prophet, but as one who was a servant of the prophet. 'But Jehoshaphat asked, "Is there no prophet of the LORD here? Let us inquire of the LORD through him." And one of the servants of the king of Israel answered, "Elisha son of Shaphat is here. He used to pour water on the hands of Elijah" (2 Kings 3:11). Look at what Elisha did. He carried a jar of water for the man of God. Whatever service you put your hands to do, do it as unto the Lord. Jesus' disciples served Him well. At some point He told them that they had surpassed the servants' mark and become friends. When they went to Antioch, they did things exactly like Christ would do and they were called Christians, meaning Christ-like. This too was through impartation.

Servanthood does not work well with a master-servant relationship, but as a father-son relationship. Elisha referred to Elijah as his father.

This is to say, his service was not forced, but out of honour, just as the Bible tells children to honour their father and mother. His service was not slavery. If you serve a person you must do it faithfully and to the end. See beyond material or monetary rewards. Gehazi would have been the next one to inherit Elisha's double portion of his spirit, but he loved Naaman's money and missed his reward.

HEALING

> *So, you shall serve the Lord you God, …I will take away sickness from among you…* (Exodus 23:25).

Another blessing that comes with service is healing. I cannot say that a servant never falls sick, but God provides healing for His servants. When snakes in the wilderness bit the children of Israel, they called on God. He neither killed the snakes nor stopped them from biting. He instructed Moses to make a bronze snake and fix it on a pole where they could see it. Whoever was bitten and looked at the snake received healing. No matter how serious a disease can be, God is healer. As long as we are in the service to the Lord, we can count on Him to heal us. In 2 Kings 20, we are told that King Hezekiah was very sick. God sent a prophet to tell him to put his house in order for he was to die. Hezekiah being a man of service, pleaded with God on the basis of his service and he was healed.

In my early days of service, I lived about seven kilometres from the church. One morning, I woke up feeling unwell and contemplated not going to church that day. I began comforting myself that God would understand I was indisposed. I turned to read my Bible and God ministered to me from Exodus 23:25,

> *and ye shall serve the Lord your God, and He shall bless thy bread, and thy water, and I will take sickness away from the midst of thee.*

This verse became very real to me that day. The Holy Spirit convicted me that there is no other medicine, no antidote that would work better than His Word. I slowly walked to the church and embarked on my work on the compound. After a few minutes, I felt power descending upon me, the peace of God overwhelmed me, and I felt the sickness leave my body. I ran into the church and began to praise God. You should have heard my testimony that day!

There was a blind woman who faithfully wiped seats in a certain church. Her children would guide her to church and she would wipe the seats before the service began. One Sunday, as she was cleaning, she heard commotion, sensing trouble and in panic, she tried to guess her way out of the church. Unfortunately, she stepped on the bucket of water and fell backwards with the water splashing over her face and body. As she wiped her face, her eyes opened. This was a miracle of service.

I have ministered in places where the people are not inclined towards service. They respond to altar calls with prayer requests for financial breakthrough, job opportunities, healing, and so forth. Every day they are prayed for but they do not see any progress. Albert Einstein said the definition of insanity is doing the same thing over and over and expecting different results! If you have prayed for breakthroughs that are not forthcoming, you need to change your prayer. Get some service to offer in the name of the LORD.

Breakthrough and Productivity

> *No one shall suffer miscarriage or be barren in your land; I will fulfil the number of your days* (Exodus 23:26).

When many people hear of miscarriage and barrenness, they imagine that it is a female's affair. This Scripture refers to more than physical miscarriage and barrenness. It is talking of breakthroughs and productivity. Servants are blessed in such a way that whatever they do succeeds. It is not the efforts of their hands, but the blessing of God. I have seen people talk against genuine pastors when they prosper.

Men too have experienced the problem of a miscarriage. Many people have trusted God for jobs and have promises for tomorrow that never come to pass. Others get good jobs but they are short-lived. Have you seen people who have done everything possible to prosper yet it seems like they are chasing the wind? They have started all manner of businesses, but they never get anything out of them? It is a form of barrenness. It is possible for anyone to miscarry in this sense. God says that if we serve Him, we will no longer experience miscarriages.

One man shared his frustrations with me. He had applied for many jobs, been invited for many interviews, and yet he still did not have a job. One day, he finally landed a job, but no sooner had he begun, than the company collapsed. He tried to set up his own business but quickly lost all his stock. One day, his landlord decided to kick him out for accumulated rent arrears. His family was out in the cold, and it is at this time he came to my office. I had great compassion for this man. Just before I laid hands on him, the Holy Spirit prompted the word 'service'. I paused and asked the man how he had been serving God. To my surprise, the brother could not trace a single thing he had done for God as a service. Instead of praying for him I gave him some assignments to do. Just as our Lord Jesus told His disciples that some demons do not go without prayer and fasting, some of our problems do not get solved without our commitment to service for God. This man was going through spiritual miscarriages. When he got involved in God's work, he prospered. Some setbacks people go through in life can be corrected through service to God.

False promises are another form of miscarriage. Many have had false promises of marriage, a job, capital to Start a business, and so forth. False promises can keep you hostage and unable to move on with life.

> *If the clouds are full of rain, they empty themselves upon the earth...* (Ecclesiastes 11:3).

Simple science tells me that clouds are formed when water evaporates and condenses in the skies. Once the condensation has taken place, at some point the clouds will break into rain. Thus, for any cloud to form, vapour must go up. In the same way, service to God can be equated to letting the vapour go up. As you keep serving God, your clouds keep forming and one day, when they are full of water, they will release the rain. I have watched athletes train for a marathon. You encounter them on the road and in their training camps training hard for the assignment ahead. You might ask what the secret to their training is. Formation of clouds is the secret behind it all. They know that when they have fully trained, the time will come for a reward.

Every person who loves sports is usually glued to the screen or packed somewhere in a stadium watching their favourite game. When winners are being interviewed, most say they prepared and practiced long and hard. Constant training is needed to form the 'clouds' of victory for them. When full of training, their clouds release victory. Beware of having a 'miscarriage'. Many people miss their blessings at the last minute. It is like an athlete who does very well along the racetrack but is defeated at the finish line. Keep serving God for you do not know when your cloud will release rain.

Promise

> *By faith Abraham, even though he was past age and Sarah herself was barren, was able to become a father because he considered Him faithful who had made the promise* (Hebrews 11:11, NIV).

In order to be most effective as a servant, you must train yourself to hear and hold on to the promises of God. These promises keep us moving and we draw our energy from them. God's promise can keep even death away. A man called Simeon had a promise that he would not die before he had seen the Lord's Christ. The moment he saw the child Jesus, he prayed that he may die. It had been revealed to him by the Holy Spirit that he would not see death before the Lord's Christ' (Luke 2:26). May you never die before enjoying your promise as a servant. The promises God made to you still hold. We need to play our part knowing that He is forever faithful, to do what He promised to do. Hang on to His promises. Servants who have known this secret are not troubled by time. They know that the promises of God are yes, and amen. The promises of God are sure. I may be growing older, but God is the same yesterday, today, and forever more.

Faithful servants in the Bible who held on to the promises of God left us a legacy to emulate. Caleb could not let go of God's promise. Although he was advanced in years, he chose to hang on what God had promised. For more than forty years he trusted God for its fruition. When Joshua divided the land that they had already captured, Caleb refused his portion. He knew that the promise of God was for a better and bigger land than the one Joshua offered.

> *Now then, just as the Lord promised, He has kept me alive for forty-five years since the time He said this to Moses, while Israel moved about in the desert. So here I*

> am today eighty-five years old. I am still as strong today as the day Moses sent men out; I am just as vigorous to go out to battle now as I was then. Now give me this hill country that the Lord promised me that day. You yourself heard then that the Anakites were there and their cities were large and fortified, but, the Lord helping me, I will drive them out just as He said. Then Joshua blessed Caleb son of Jephunneh and gave him Hebron as his inheritance (Joshua 14:10-13).

Caleb's promise had taken forty-five years to come to pass, but it was very fresh in his mind. Age never spoke to him, it was just a number. He knew that the promises of God are true. Why was he so determined to take the mountain? What was so special about that particular hill that he desired? Why could he not settle for the already conquered land? Many people like to settle in territory that has already been conquered. They do not want to fight for more land. They are comfortable with what they have. Like a pioneer, Caleb wanted to keep on conquering. Corporate blessings did not move his heart.

People in developing countries get excited when they hear that the IMF (International Monetary Fund) or World Bank is releasing financial aid to their country. Even people who do not understand the meaning of it, talk about it and celebrate. It is okay to feel good, but how much of these funds can one take home for food? The government will get the money, but individual citizens will still go hungry or thirsty. Corporate blessings may not translate into tangible personal benefit. Caleb was not moved by this kind of blessing. He trusted God to capture a hill country for his inheritance. When everybody else scrambled for small pieces of land in the already congested plateaus, Caleb distinguished himself as a man who knew and understood the promises of God.

> **Reflection**
>
> a. What stands out for you in this chapter?
>
> b. What will you begin to do differently in your service to God based on what you have read from this chapter?

CONCLUSION

God is looking for people who are willing to serve him sacrificially. In other words, people who are willing to die to self and to be inconvenienced, not for what they would gain, but for the glory of God. As we serve, we must always remember that God is not short of alternatives; serving Him is a privilege. In order for one to be the servant God is looking for, they must allow God to mould them by following the principles and the practical lessons shared in this book. It is prudent to note that reading this book does not make one a servant. It is putting into practice the lessons learnt that shapes the reader into a sacrificial servant.

I will conclude this book with some reflections drawn from the following Scriptures.

> *Then Jesus lifted up His eyes, and seeing a great multitude coming towards Him, He said to Philip, 'Where shall we buy bread that these may eat?' But this He said to test him, for He Himself knew what He would do. Philip answered Him, 'Two hundred denarii worth of bread is not sufficient for them, that every one of them may have a little.' One of His disciples Andrew, Simon Peter's brother, said to Him. 'There is a lad here who*

> *has five barley loaves and two small fish, but what are they among so many?'* (John 6:5-6)

God has a plan

Always remember that God has a plan for what He will do. Many times He will demand a lot from you, but by knowing that there is a purpose and a plan brings comfort and encouragement. Philip did calculations for Jesus. Perhaps he was an accountant. No wonder he quickly offered them a solution to their predicament. We need such people in ministry who can provide solutions without hesitation. Nevertheless, when it comes to responding to God, we must not think twice. We know that nothing is impossible with Him and that He has a solution to all our problems. Andrew was just a simple man and a true servant. He knew that nothing was too hard for God. When he saw a boy with five loaves and two fishes he realised there was some possibility there for Jesus to use. A true servant does not see impossibilities in God. Even in a wilderness, God will provide some fish and loaves of bread to carry you through.

The time to serve is now

There is no convenient time or place for service. Some young people have told me that they will serve after they get married; married people tell me that they will serve when their children are older; students say when they secure a job they will serve; while those working are convinced they are too busy working to serve. The Bible says that whoever waits for a perfect time does nothing (Ecclesiastes 11:4). I challenge you to respond to this call of service and do that which God has called you to do. There is no superior service; it is about the One you serve not what you do. Elisha poured water on the hands of Elijah. He was not his driver or his accountant, yet he did it so well and faithfully that he received his reward.

Favour factor

My academic background is in accounting. One time, I heard from a friend that a local company had advertised for a position of an accountant, so I presented myself for an interview. I had prayed for God's favour that morning and also prayed over my certificates. When my turn came, I was called in. I had just shut the door behind me, when the company's manager shouted, 'What do you want in my office?' 'I have come to interview for the job you advertised,' I replied shocked at his outburst. His next words were even worse, 'You do not qualify to be talking to me, let alone working for me. Get out!' I had never faced such a rude person before. As I began to walk out of his office, the Holy Spirit spoke to me and said I should take courage and tell him something about myself.

Turning back, I said, 'Excuse me sir, why do you think I can't work for you?'

'Because that's what your papers say,' he said.

I went closer to him and said, 'I appreciate your observation, but please set those papers aside and I will tell you what is not reflected in them. If you employ me you will get a good man, but if you don't, you will miss an excellent man. Thank you.'

As I turned to walk out, the man called my name and asked, 'Are you born again?'

'Yes' I replied. In summary, I got the job, despite the fact that I was the least qualified among the interviewees. This could only be the favour factor.

BIBLIOGRAPHY

Abelly, Louis. *The Life of the Venerable Servant of God, Vincent de Paul*. New City Press, 1993.

Apple, Michael W. *Educating the Right Way: Markets, Standards, God, and Inequality*. Routledge, 2013.

Armstrong, Karen. *A Story of God: The 4,000-Year Quest of Judaism, Christianity and Islam*. Ballantine Books, 2011.

Asante, Samuel Kwesi. *Process and Qualities for Developing Servant-shepherd Leaders Within the Church of Pentecost for Effective Cross-cultural Ministry*. Oral Roberts University, 2005.

Benson, Taft. 'Whom The Lord Calls He Qualifies'. Retrieved from http://media.ldscdn.org/pdf/magazines/ensign-july-2013/2013-07-05-whom-the-lord-calls-he-qualifies-eng.pdf. [Accessed: 02/07/2020].

Bruns, J. Edgar. 'The Servant of God'. *Studies in Biblical Theology* 20 (1957): 535-538.

Chung, Young Soo. 'Why Servant Leadership? Its Uniqueness and Principles in the Life of Jesus.' *Journal of Asia Adventist Seminary* 14, no. 2 (2011).

Cosgrove, Francis. 'The Disciple Is a Servant'. *Discipleship Journal* 30 (1985): 35-36. Retrieved from https://static1.squarespace.com/static/530e4ef9e4b07ec5e7d89c14/t/570e79b4e32140b109eb-9cae/1460566452718/The+Disciple+is+a+Servant+-+Francis+Cosgrove.pdf. [Accessed: 02/05/2020].

Dennis, Robert S., and Mihai Bocarnea. 'Development of the Servant Leadership Assessment Instrument'. *Leadership & Organization Development Journal* (2005).

Eyring, Henry B. *Rise to Your Call*. (2002). Retrieved from http://www.sandysports.org/uploads/1/7/2/9/17295724/rise_to_your_call_-_henry_b._eyring.pdf. [Accessed: 02/07/2020.]

Gonen, Rivka. *Contested Holiness: Jewish, Muslim, and Christian Perspectives on the Temple Mount in Jerusalem*. KTAV Publishing House, Inc., 2003.

Henry, Matthew, and Leslie F. Church. *Commentary on the Whole Bible*. Zondervan Publishing House, 1961.

Herman, Harvey A. *Discipleship by Design*. Xulon Press, 2008.

Hillyer, Norman. "The Servant of God." *Evangelical Quarterly* 41 (1969): 143-60. Retrieved from https://biblicalstudies.org.uk/pdf/eq/1969-3_143.pdf. [Accessed: 02/06/2020].

Howell, Don N. *Servants of the Servant: A Biblical Theology of Leadership*. Wipf and Stock Publishers, 2003.

Hyers, Conrad. *The Comic Vision and the Christian Faith: A Celebration of Life and Laughter*. Wipf and Stock Publishers, 2003.

Illff, Gayle S. *Succeeding as a New Convert*. Retrieved from http://media.ldscdn.org/pdf/magazines/ensign-february-2009/2009-02-07-succeeding-as-a-new-convert-eng.pdf. [Accessed: 02/06/2020.]

Kadalie, David. *Leaders' Resource Kit: Tools and Techniques to Develop your Leadership*. Evangel Publishing House, 2006.

Kostenberger, Andreas. *Marriage, and Family: Rebuilding the Biblical Foundation*. Wheaton: Crossway (2004).

Lawson, James Gregory. *Patterns of Discipleship in the New Testament as Evidenced by Jesus and Peter*. Southwestern Baptist Theological Seminary, 2013.

Lynch, JA & Friedman, HH. 'Servant Leader, Spiritual Leader: The Case for Convergence'. *Journal of Leadership, Accountability and Ethics* 10, no. 2 (2013): 87-95.

Maciariello, Joseph. 'Lessons in Leadership and Management from Nehemiah'. *Theology Today* 60, no. 3 (2003): 397-407.

Meyer, Frederick Brotherton. *Moses: The Servant of God*. FH Revell Company, 1894.

Ogden, Greg, and Daniel Meyer. *Leadership Essentials: Shaping Vision, Multiplying Influence, Defining Character*. InterVarsity Press, 2009.

Payne, David F. 'The Servant of the Lord: Language and Interpretation'. *Evangelical Quarterly* 43 (1971): 131-43.

Pope, Randy. *Insourcing: Bringing Discipleship Back to the Local Church*. Zondervan, 2013.

Rainey, Anson F. 'The Order of Sacrifices in Old Testament Ritual Texts.' *Biblica* 51, no. 4 (1970): 485-498.

Ward, James M. 'The Servant Songs in Isaiah.' *Review & Expositor* 65, no. 4 (1968): 433-446.

Wiersbe, Warren W. *On Being a Servant of God*. Baker Books, 2007.

Willard, Dallas. *Hearing God: Developing a Conversational Relationship with God*. InterVarsity Press, 2012.

Williams, John Rodman. *Renewal theology: Systematic Theology from a Charismatic Perspective*. Harper Collins, 1996.

ABOUT THE AUTHOR

Apostle Patrick Murithii Nyaga is the lead minister of the Gospel Celebration Church, Nairobi. He trained and worked as an ac-countant before joining full-time ministry. Patrick holds a Bachelor of Arts in Bible and Theology degree from Pan Africa Christian University. In addition to his role as a lead minister, he is also a global conference speaker and regularly contributes articles in the Leadership Journal and Leadership Today Africa. He also has a television program, "Called to Serve" on Kingdom Television, in Kenya. Patrick is married to Grace, and they are blessed with three children, Jewel, Moses, and Collins.

OTHER BOOKS BY THE AUTHOR

Every Leader's Battle: Experiences, Encouragement & Lessons from 10 Leaders

Money Matters: Spiritual Foundation, Principles & Practical Application

Leadership Pitfalls: Mistakes Every Leader Must Avoid (Amharic Translation)

Leadership Pitfalls: Mistakes Every Leader Must Avoid

CALLED TO SERVE (Amharic Translation)

Contacts:

✉ pmnyagah@gmail.com

📞 +254722584660

f Apostle Patrick Muriithi Nyaga

www.amazon.com

Made in the USA
Middletown, DE
10 November 2024